Authority and Anglicanism

Authority and Anglicanism

Stephen Ross White

SCM PRESS LTD

0 334 02631 8

First published 1996
by SCM Press Ltd
9–17 St Albans Place, London N1 0NX

Printed in Great Britain by
Biddles Ltd, Guildford and King's Lynn

Contents

Introduction

A number of books have appeared in recent years which have attempted to articulate something of the essence of Anglicanism or to relate Anglicanism to some of the issues and opportunities confronting the wider church. The best of these books have been by some extremely distinguished church figures and theologians such as Archbishop Michael Ramsey, Bishop Stephen Sykes and G.R. Evans. As long ago as 1978 in *The Integrity of Anglicanism* Stephen Sykes set out to deal with what he later called 'the question of liberalism and comprehensiveness',[1] and more recently in *Unashamed Anglicanism* (a book to which we shall be making substantial reference in this study) he has identified a number of areas, including those of ecclesiology and authority, which have concerned him for many years,[2] and to which Anglicanism needs to pay serious attention if it is to maintain – or perhaps regain – its coherence and distinctive identity as a viable ecclesial family. In a somewhat different vein G. R. Evans has paid detailed attention to the problems surrounding the exercise of authority *within* the church, taking as a starting point three areas of controversy arising in connection with the church's own internal authority structures. Of these:

The first concerns the style of such 'exercising' of authority, whether it is to compel obedience or constitute any kind of dominion; whether it should resemble contemporary political government in its shape and

1

methods of administration. The second has to do with the particular types of 'officer' the 'society' of the Church should have. The third involves the relationship between the ministry of the whole people of God and the ministry of these 'officers'.[3]

In each case these authors have sought to root their thinking in a long tradition of Anglican theology, and have examined in some detail their particular areas of concern. By contrast, this study is more general in its scope and in its argument. It is not intended as a rival work of scholarship in the overtly learned tradition of such figures, and for this reason footnotes and references have been kept to a minimum. Rather, it is intended for the more general – though also the informed – reader, and it is less of a scholarly monograph and more of an appreciation and critique of Anglicanism from the perspective of one thinking, praying Anglican who is himself deeply committed to the daily round of Anglican parish life.

From such a perspective there appears to have been, increasingly in recent years, something of a crisis of confidence and identity within Anglicanism. As a communion, and certainly within particular provinces such as the Church of England, our Anglican identity has been eroded by a number of factors, historical, structural, critical and moral, and these will be examined in some detail in the first chapters of this book. To a large extent this erosion has coincided with a period of declining membership, although I suspect that this is in fact a symptom rather than a cause of uncertainty. It has also coincided with a number of particularly heated debates about various issues of church order within the Anglican communion and these, I believe, are equally a symptom of a renewed, but fundamentally misplaced, search for identity. John Hick distinguishes between what he calls 'penultimate' and 'ultimate' issues,[4] and in a different context this distinction is useful here. Thus these debates over such matters of order as the ordination of women are, I believe, attempts to establish identity on matters of only penultimate importance, and the heat generated by such debates is a symptom of that identity's having been lost – or at least obscured – on issues of ultimate importance. This is a problem to which Stephen Sykes pays a good deal of attention in his latest book, *Unashamed Anglicanism*. He identifies the ultimate issue as being the almost wilful refusal of Anglicanism to articulate a distinctive Anglican ecclesiology, and argues that this creates problems both within the communion and in the ecumenical arena:

> We have to face the uncomfortable fact that traditional Anglican diffidence in presenting its doctrine of the Church....strikes Christians of other allegiances not as the fruit of modesty, but of pride and fear: pride, in desiring to occupy a place which no other communion in Christendom occupies, and fear of the consequences, internal and external, of having to formulate a responsible account on behalf of a body which has got out of the habit of taking its theology seriously.[5]

In the same context he quotes the Inter-Anglican Theological and Doctrinal Commission:

> For too long Anglicans have appeared willing to evade responsible theological reflection and dialogue by acquiescing automatically and immediately in the coexistence of incompatible views, opinions and policies.[6]

Anglicanism has, it appears, brought many of its problems on itself by using penultimate issues as a means of running away from the ultimate issue of Anglican identity and ecclesiology. Thus in the absence of any thoroughgoing

Anglican doctrine of the church the various penultimate issues have gradually assumed greater and greater importance during the last generation or so, and Anglicanism has found itself rocked by a variety of debates both theological and practical – debates which are all the more destructive because of the absence of any solid Anglican theological context in which to conduct them. As these debates have undermined the confidence of the church still further, so, in an increasingly vicious circle, things penultimate have come to dominate the theological, liturgical and practical agendas of the communion.

Anglicanism, it must be admitted, is particularly prone to such debates and to the potential for damage inherent within them. It is so precisely, and ironically, as a result of some of its greatest strengths – its tolerance and liberality. It is neither sufficiently hierarchical (or authoritarian), nor sufficiently biblically fundamentalist (for the most part at least) to be able simply to suppress any inconvenient or uncomfortable debates before they begin; and once they have begun it has no knock-down scriptural or *ex cathedra* arguments with which to annihilate the dissidents. In this connection it is interesting – though also distressing – to note that it is precisely those sections of the Anglican Church which are most fundamentalist in outlook which are (in common with some of the smaller fundamentalist churches and the ever increasing number of house churches) growing and proclaiming a real identity even at the present time. One may not care overmuch for their identity, but one is forced to admit that they have one! Such groups pronounce what is and is not permissible on *a priori* grounds, and will not tolerate any deviation from that norm. Such groups are thankfully, however, the exception rather than the rule within Anglicanism.

A further factor which has contributed to this problem of identity for Anglicanism is its exposure to the harsh and

4

Introduction

bitter winds of public opinion. As a communion the Anglican Church believes – even where it is not the Established Church – that it is a part of the community in which it is set, and not a holy or exclusive huddle, and this stance, though again admirable, makes it especially vulnerable to whatever influences are at work in any particular society. It has found itself, therefore, more exposed than most of the main-line churches to the complex moral debates which have surfaced throughout society during recent years. What should be its attitude towards divorce and re-marriage in church? To homosexuality among either lay people or clergy? To unemployment? To civil unrest? To euthanasia and to abortion?

The problem is further compounded by the fact that whatever the church chooses to say – or not to say – about such issues as these will inevitably arouse a storm of criticism from one quarter or another. If the church maintains a discreet silence it is weak or divorced from the real world; if it espouses even a moderately liberal viewpoint it is 'trendy' or subversive; and if it speaks with a more conservative voice it is 'mediaeval', 'repressive' or 'reactionary'. Perhaps the most obvious example of this hyper-critical attitude towards the church has been the response of government to criticism from church leaders. In principle politicians – especially Conservative ones – have frequently called on the church to provide a moral lead in society and to take a place in the life of the nation. However, as soon as church leaders voice an opinion which is critical of government policy on some social issue or other, the church is told that it has no business meddling with politics and should stick to its own affairs and not tell other people how to conduct theirs! Or perhaps at best it is told that it should speak out on personal moral issues but keep silent on social ones which it does not understand. In such a critical atmosphere it is small wonder that the church should sometimes appear to be in two minds about how to think and act.

Faced with these problems, and with – as we shall see in ensuing chapters – an acute dilemma as to what model or style of authority it can exert or aspire to possess, there are all too often only two poles of response. Each of them certainly provides the church with an identity, but it is seriously open to question whether this identity is in the best interests either of the church itself, or of the world which the church is, presumably, there to serve.

The first option is for the church to cut itself off from the world and to become either a 'holy huddle' or a club for the like-minded. Such a response to tribulation has a long history from the Patristic era onwards,[7] and reached its zenith in the two or three centuries following the Reformation as the Protestant churches over much of Europe split again and again, each smaller and smaller sect proclaiming itself to be the one true church and holier than all of the rest. It must be admitted that there is still a strong temptation to follow this path today. It is no accident that many Irish towns, for example, have 'First' and 'Second' Presbyterian Churches, and there are local congregations within Anglicanism, especially at the extreme Anglo-Catholic and Evangelical ends of the spectrum, who do seem primarily concerned to construct a small enclave of holiness without much regard for what is taking place in the world outside the four walls of the church building and its 'Holy Fellowship'.

Attractive though this option may sometimes appear, there are a number of cogent theological and ecclesiological objections to it. To begin with, it involves the judgment of one part of the church by another. That is, the exclusive arrogation of holiness to oneself involves the denial of it in others, and as St Augustine argued against the Donatists, this has always been a flaw in every attempt to establish an

'extra holy' church or church-within-a-church. According to
the more classical doctrine expounded by such figures as
Cyprian and Augustine of Hippo, the church is, and will
always be, a mixed community of saints and sinners. Even if
one holds the extreme Cyprianite position of *extra ecclesiam
nulla salus*, it does not follow that because there is no
salvation outside the church, therefore all within it are
automatically saved, or even especially holy! According to
this position, we are not equipped to judge who is and who
is not within the fold of the communion of saints. Our part
is only to welcome all and sundry into the visible church,
and leave it to God to weed out the wheat from the chaff in
his own time and fashion.

Secondly, the setting up of a church apart from the world
and apart from others who would also claim to be a part of
the church entails a wilful division and separation not only
from the world, but also from those parts of the church
which see it as their mission and calling to remain involved
with the world. It is very difficult to maintain a balance
between standing apart and standing aloof, and historically
not many – if indeed any – attempts to walk this particular
tightrope have been successful. It is perhaps in recognition
of this potential imbalance that even many closed religious
orders (to take the most extreme example of isolation from
the world) have, whilst rightly remaining devoted primarily
to the pursuit of holiness, nonetheless re-opened
negotiations with the world and found a new vocation in
some form of direct service to that world, and in a greater
connection than previously with the rest of the church. A
living connection with the whole body of the church is
necessary for any congregation or order which takes
seriously Jesus' call to unity as well as his warnings against
the dangers involved in judging others.

Thirdly, a holiness which keeps itself determinedly aloof
from the world is in danger of denying, implicitly even if not

explicitly, one of the key doctrinal motifs of the Christian faith, namely the incarnation. Whether one's interpretation of the incarnation is conservative or radical, literal or metaphorical, the practical implications of the doctrine remain substantially the same. Thus any form of the doctrine of the incarnation assumes that we have to do with a God who is intimately and passionately concerned for the well-being of his creation, and especially of his people. And this doctrinal basis is borne out by even the most cursory glance at the life and ministry of Jesus himself, a ministry which, according to St Luke's Gospel, Jesus himself characterized as being in the active prophetic mould:

The scroll of the prophet Isaiah was handed to him. Unrolling it, he found the place where it is written: 'The Spirit of the Lord is on me, because he has anointed me to preach good news to the poor, He has sent me to proclaim freedom for the prisoners and recovery of sight for the blind, to release the oppressed, to proclaim the year of the Lord's favour.'[8]

In his working out of this 'manifesto' during the course of his ministry, it would be hard, on the evidence of the Gospels, to present Jesus as a recluse, or as one who was more concerned for his own holiness than for the people among whom he taught and preached. Certainly he is recorded as having needed periods of solitude and silence for prayer and for rest, but those periods were sought precisely in order to enable him then to return to the milling crowds and the needy individuals. Likewise, he is presented as listening to the needs of those who came to him even when his disciples might have preferred him to ignore this particular blind man or social outcast and come away to be 'holy' with them.

If Christianity is credibly to claim to follow such a figure, and to accept at whatever level that this involvement of

Jesus with the society of his time (and frequently the less salubrious elements of that society) reflects something of the nature of God and his response to his creation, then it cannot, without making a mockery of this claim, ever turn its back on the world or seek to save its own soul at the expense of the 'sinners' and 'outcasts' whom Jesus came to serve and to save. Any church or congregation which cuts itself off from the world in this way not only sets itself up in unwarranted judgment over others and promotes hurt and dissension but also, and most damagingly, forfeits its claim to faithfulness to the pattern of Christ's ministry and to the mind of Christ himself.

The second option which the church can take as its response to the world is that of straightforward denunciation of the world and its standards. Occasionally renunciation and denunciation may, of course, overlap, but I am thinking here primarily of those occasions on which the church has not cut itself off from the world, but rather stood, as it were, in the market place and castigated the world for its sins and proclaimed that the individual's only hope of salvation lies in catching hold of the lifebelt of faith before he sinks without trace in the morass of society's wickedness.

Again, this response to the world might have its superficial attractions, in that it does provide the church with an identity of the 'ark of salvation' variety. Again, however, there are serious reservations concerning such an understanding of the church and of faith.

First, it again involves judgment, just as much as the 'holy huddle' variety of church life does, and it invokes this judgment in a naive and simplistic manner which suggests that society is 'bad' whilst the church is 'good'. No one would pretend that the world of business, international affairs, politics and so on is spotless in its purity – one glance at the morning paper on the breakfast table is enough to dispel that illusion – but neither is it wholly or irredeemably bad. Within this same world, though rarely making the headlines, there are the compelling examples of honesty, compassion, self-sacrifice and generosity of spirit which make sweeping judgments unfounded, and there are many men and women who endeavour to conduct their business and personal lives with an integrity which the church itself would sometimes do well to notice and to emulate.

Equally, the church becomes guilty of blatant hypocrisy the moment it claims that it is unequivocally 'good'. If it were, it would not be divided, the vicar would never run off with the organist's wife, the treasurer would never cook the books, and several million pounds would never disappear from ECUSA's funds! It is not so much the fact of judgment as its naivety or hypocrisy which makes the equation of society and the church with wickedness and goodness respectively so repugnant to the moral sensibilities of Christianity, and so repellent and offensive to non-Christians.

Secondly, any wholesale or blanket denunciation of the failings of society denies that there is any overlap between the church and society, and thereby induces a kind of religious schizophrenia in the believer. Indeed, it is hard to see how one could live a tolerable life if condemned forever to have a foot in both camps. One may be part of the 'good' church on Sunday, but one is inexorably thrown back into the 'bad' world for the rest of the week through the simple expedients of earning a living, running a home, going shopping and so on. If in response to the problem you sit light to these various worldly employments, then ninety per cent of life is implicitly devalued and one's daily round is threatened with meaninglessness; and if on the other hand you immerse yourself in these pursuits then the unity of life is threatened by the radical disjuction between this side of your life and the side which the church proclaims as valid.

Thirdly, the attitude of denunciation proves to be no less false to the pattern of Christ himself than an attitude of separation is. It denies not so much the doctrine of the incarnation in itself, but more the characteristic mode of Jesus' activity. It fails to take account of his inexhaustible compassion for the frailties and sins of those around him, and it ignores the insight that Jesus changed people's lives far more often by calling them and leading them gently on in love than he did by shrieking denunciation at them – indeed, it is interesting that on the rare occasions he denounced anyone, it was usually the self-professedly 'holy' religious leaders that were his target!

For all these reasons, then, and also because both attitudes deny a fundamental response to the creation as 'good' (thereby failing to maintain the necessary balance between salvationist and creationist views of theology and ethics), I regard neither withdrawal nor denunciation as an adequate response to the problems which the modern world poses to the church. This book is therefore written in the belief that for Anglicanism there *does* remain another way forward. More precisely, it is written in the belief that it can and *must* re-assert (indeed, if Stephen Sykes is right, re-discover and re-articulate) its identity, and that it has a potentially valuable role to play in the shaping of our society and our world precisely in what I shall argue is its capacity to combine moderation and a modified approach to authority. I have written simply as one who is striving to find and articulate what Anglicanism has to offer today, and for all those who feel, however obscurely, that there is a jewel within Anglicanism which both the wider church and the world lose or ignore at their peril. To all those who seek, therefore, in Stephen Sykes' immortal phrase, 'The Integrity of Anglicanism', this book is dedicated and offered.

1

Historical Authority

I

We have argued that much of the trauma which Anglicanism is suffering at the present time is related to a weakened sense of its own identity. This is, as we have seen, partly self-inflicted and partly an almost inevitable consequence of Anglicanism's laudable unwillingness to separate itself from an often sceptical and critical world. This weakening of identity has contributed also to a crisis of authority within the church, and although the two issues cannot be kept entirely separate, it is with the particular problem of authority rather than with the wider problem of identity that I am primarily concerned in this study. Furthermore, whilst other writers, and among them recently G.R. Evans, have dealt with authority *within* the church – in other words with its own systems of government, its 'officers' and so on – I propose to examine here the slightly different concept of the authority *of* the church. By this phrase is meant whatever claim the church feels able to make about the status of its teaching and its life-style, for the church does not just go its own way according to its own internal rules, but rather it has, in every age, proclaimed both its doctrines, its worship and its practices as being potentially applicable to everyone, and it has preached and taught in God's name and challenged the world with his call to all people. Today, as a part of the wider crisis of identity, this sense of the church's authority in the world is under threat, and the question is being posed as to exactly what kind of authority, if any, (and based on what foundation) the church can reasonably claim to possess.

Thus we may ask the question: What therefore have been the traditional sources of authority within Anglicanism, and particularly within the Church of England, and why have these declined in efficacy to the point where they have ceased to function in the ways they undoubtedly once did? Perhaps these sources may be conveniently grouped under four general headings: historical authority; structural authority; biblical and credal authority; and moral authority. These will be examined in turn in this and the succeeding three chapters, and we shall then consider in chapter 5 how it is that their demise had led to a crisis of authority within Anglicanism.

The phrase 'historical authority' is used here to denote a cluster of ideas which have, either explicitly or implicitly, contributed to supporting the traditional authority of the church, especially in England. Few of these ideas are strictly ecclesiological or theological in origin, but they have not been any the less powerful for that. Indeed, they are a reflection of the long standing and complex relationship between the church and the state (in the broadest sense) in England, and of the ways in which the church has received a kind of vicarious authority by means of this relationship.

It is a relationship which stems from the founding of Anglicanism, and from the morass of mixed motives and political and religious bickering between England and Rome which led to Henry VIII and his successors being styled 'Supreme Head of the Church' and 'Defender of the Faith'. Too much has been written on all sides regarding the 'rightness' or 'wrongness' of Henry's actions, and in spite of all this it is still open to dispute as to whether the founding of Anglicanism was the result of a sincere faith or political determination or personal opportunism, or, indeed, an inextricable and possibly unholy mixture of all three! Whatever the reasons behind it may have been, it is the simple fact of royal involvement and leadership which is significant for our purposes, for this inevitably facilitated an early sense of authority for at least two reasons.

First, the authority imparted by the mere presence of monarchy in the ecclesiastical world. This may not ever have been an entirely unmixed blessing as far as the church was concerned, but its efficacy in terms of creating a power structure for the church had been demonstrated time and again ever since the first involvement of the Emperor Constantine in church affairs and government. In the break with Rome, then, Henry and his successors had effectively asserted their power in both the secular and the sacred realms, and for many people there would have been a sense that Henry and 'his' church were the new religious rulers who must be obeyed. Certainly over the next century or so, until the situation finally settled down and the Church of England became the Established Church, monarchs had few scruples about using their secular power in defence of their religious beliefs, and those who deviated from the accepted pattern of belief found for themselves just how ruthless the combined authority of church and state could be. It would be hard to argue that this monarchical authority – linked as it was to the exercise of coercion – was a blessing to the church, but it did undoubtedly provide a foundation for its authority, and similarly helps us to see the Church of England as being set in the context of a genuine (if also harsh and dictatorial) authority structure right from its inception.

We must be careful too not to judge this kind of authority over simplistically and harshly through the medium of our twentieth-century fondness for democracy and self-determination in matters of conscience. We may view with some mistrust a monarchical model of church authority, but for many people at the time (and especially given the traditional insularity of the English character) this authority would have been welcomed with gratitude since it was 'home based', and no longer dependent on the validation of the Bishop of Rome. Henry's authority was, one suspects, all the more effective because it was not merely imposed from outside – as the Pope's had necessarily been – but actively approved of as producing a new and meaningful national and ecclesiastical identity.

Secondly, there was the authority which the church itself derived from this association with the monarchy. The presence of the monarch at the head of the newly reformed church imparted an immediate and all-pervading power-structure to that church. Again, I am far from arguing that this was necessarily beneficial, but merely that it happened. The hierarchy of King/Archbishops/Bishops/Clergy/People provided a neat and tidy chain of command in which everyone knew their place, and the church was thus conveniently slotted into the generally authoritarian and power-oriented ethos of society. It reflected the same structures and it therefore wielded a comparable power. The authority of the church may have been derived at second hand from that of the monarch, but it was nonetheless real for that.

It would be easy to overplay the importance of Reformation politics and the role of the monarch in creating the identity of the Church of England, and already more than enough of both praise and blame have been allotted to Henry for the outcome of the Reformation in England. Equally, however, the significance of the alliance between church and state should not be underestimated, and it is interesting that it may be cogently argued that the only other area of Europe where the Reformation Church established such a hegemony was in Calvin's Geneva, where this alliance, although forged between the city fathers and the church rather than between a monarch and the church, was equally all-encompassing.

Regardless of the various opinions which may be held regarding the English Reformation, however, it is incontrovertible that the association of the monarchy with the church did – and until relatively recently has continued to – invest the church with a sense both of its own dignity and importance and also a definite power structure, never a precisely defined one perhaps, but still a potent one. As the absolute authority of the monarchy has declined, so too has that of the church, but until the last few decades there was still a sense that the ethos of the church was one which found it natural to govern and in which the exercise of authority was a normal and accepted part of life.

Flowing from this direct involvement with the monarchy is the more complex issue of the relationship between the church and the state as a whole. At one level this has been – and still is, in England at least – simply that of an Established Church: a church with a certain position *vis-a-vis* the state, a position which carries with it both rights and responsibilities; the right, for example, for certain bishops to sit in the House of Lords, and the responsibility to crown monarchs and to minister to the spiritual life and officiate at the public celebrations of the Royal family. Clearly there is again in this a certain tendency towards the gaining of power on the part of the church, but I am far from certain that this is ultimately the most significant aspect of the relationship in terms of the authority of the church. More enduringly pervasive than the simple existence of the relationship, and more productive of power and authority, has been the church's response to this relationship – a response in which the potential for authority has been deftly, if not always righteously, maximized. Thus for the greater part of its history, and with relatively rare exceptions, the response of the church – or at least of the more influential parts of it – to is privileged position in the state has been to uphold the life of that state as represented in the government, laws, customs and social mores of any particular era – in other words to present itself as the great upholder of the *status quo*, and thereby earn the affection of the powers within the state for whom that same *status quo* is the most comfortable option. Perhaps the most blatant popular example of this upholding of 'the way things are' is to be found in the celebrated (and now thankfully excised) verse from Mrs Cecil Frances Alexander's hymn, *All things bright and beautiful*:

> The rich man in his castle,
> The poor man at his gate,
> God made them, high or lowly,
> And ordered their estate.

Such an attitude in turn fostered a belief within the church of its own divinely ordained authority. Not only did the church hold a privileged position in the life of the nation, but it was right that it should do so, and right also that it should exercise the power which God had given to it. It is small wonder that so many of the great reforms of society during the eighteenth and nineteenth centuries were pioneered by nonconformists and Quakers rather than by Anglicans, whose unspoken but heartfelt motto might well have been, 'Whatever is, is right.'[1]

Such an attitude on the part of church and society (or at least that part of society which wielded all the influence and power) was bound to be circular and self-protecting. Thus it is no surprise to find that for many years the majority of the clergy – and almost all of the senior clergy – came from the ranks of the landed and upper classes, and that they themselves fed and fostered this perception of the church as a wielder of both sacred and social power. Indeed, even such an enlightened figure as Sydney Smith writes approvingly of the genteel authority of the clergy, describing himself in Foston as 'village parson, village doctor, village comforter, village magistrate and Edinburgh Reviewer',[2] and the list of his friends and acquaintances reads like an early-nineteenth-century edition of *Who's Who*. Likewise bishops tended to be connected with – and often related to – those who governed the country or at least owned the major part of its resources and land, and the church was seen, rightly or wrongly, as enjoying all the advantages of its liaison with the state, and indeed until the repeal of the Test and Corporation Acts and the passing of the Catholic Emancipation Act these advantages were not merely the more intangible ones of prestige and influence, but also the eminently practical ones of employment and education.

II

We have examined, at least briefly, some of the more overt and structured connections between the church and the state, and traced the historical consequences of those connections as far as the power of the church is concerned, but the ramifications of the church/state relationship extend far beyond its more obvious manifestations and consequences. The significance of this relationship has never depended merely upon the legal and constitutional links between church and state. Underpinning these links there has always been also a much more nebulous and disparate – though very emotive – sense of the place of the church within the life of the nation. This has not been entirely dependent upon, although it is to a certain extent bound up with, the more formal position of the church as 'Established by Law', and it has worked itself out and shown itself not so much in the major issues of national life as in the day-to-day life of local communities throughout the ages.

Regardless, then, of such concrete manifestations of the church/state relationship as the existence of an Established Church and bishops sitting in the House of Lords, there has been, for many centuries, a perception and a belief that the church is, and for the most part should be, at the heart of society. Since long before the Reformation church buildings had tended to be built at the centre of a community (frequently, indeed, a monastic foundation was the original settlement in an area), and this physical siting of the church was an acted symbol of the place of that church in the life of the community. In this sense the Church of England merely inherited and maintained this central position, although during the nineteenth century it also developed it as new churches were built at the heart of new centres of population during the industrial revolution. The fact that these churches did not always succeed in touching the majority of the local population is irrelevant – their mere presence is a symbol of the church's vision of itself as being not only a part of, but also the bedrock of society.

In other respects, however, there were significant post-Reformation developments which served to foster the dominance of the church within society. Thus increasingly, and then around the late seventeenth century completely, the church was responsible for maintaining records of births (or at least, of baptisms, which at that period in history amounted to much the same thing), marriages and deaths, long before central government had developed the resources to register these events adequately. People were led, therefore, to see the church as presiding over these events in a secular as well as in a sacred fashion. Life, at all its most important points, was referred to the church, and it was plain that these events could only be socially acceptable when they were hallowed by the church. If the church refused this hallowing, as in the case of refusing to bury a suicide in consecrated ground, then all the stigma of 'unholiness' (or, perhaps, even more strongly 'damnation') became attached to it, and, in this case, suicide became not merely a crime, but a subject of social taboo and moral repugnance until well into the present century.

Similarly, and also through its power over people at these points in their lives, the Established Church could exert considerable leverage over people in their personal lives. For example, in Ireland before the various Emancipation Acts (and occasionally even after them) Church of Ireland registers of marriage will often record the marriage of two Roman Catholics (unflatteringly referred to as 'papists' in the registers), marriage in the then still Established Church of Ireland being the only marriage which was likely to be socially acceptable among those whose favour must needs be curried.

Likewise, the church had no scruples about pronouncing moral judgment on all issues and on all who deviated from its own norms of behaviour. My own cathedral parish records bear the word 'illegitimate' over a good one-fifth of eighteenth-century baptismal records, and successive parish curates had little hesitation in pronouncing people to be 'vagrants', 'beggars' and the like, even when, as in the case of burials, no reference to their manner of life was required in the register. In terms of people's daily lives, and the way in which they thought of themselves, there is no doubt that for several centuries the church exercised a good deal of influence – and at times outright power – over the lives of much of the population.

By no means all of the church's influence and authority has been based on such a dubious foundation as that of moral judgement, however. The church also, and especially from the mid-eighteenth-century onwards, has a consistent and at times a highly commendable record in the realm of social progress and betterment, whether merely through encouragement or through more direct means of involvement. This involvement in no way runs counter to the church's equally strong interest in preserving the *status quo* to which we alluded earlier. Thus the Established Church has frequently fought shy of major social upheaval or radical change which might seem to threaten this ordered fabric of society, but it has been willing to work assiduously to better the conditions of particular classes or groups within it. The abolition of the slave trade in the eighteenth century and the reform of prison conditions in the nineteenth century may have been too radical for the Established Church, with the notable exception of a few independently-minded individuals, but the church of England could and did involve itself in a wide variety of other, and equally vital social projects, most notably perhaps in the fields of medicine and education. It may be argued that this involvement was not undertaken for entirely altruistic motives, in that it is more than possible that the alleviation of conditions for the poor was one means of averting major social upheaval and therefore actually of preserving the *status quo*, but this possibility does not affect the fact that the church's involvement in these fields represented a major contribution to the cementing of its place at the heart of the nation's life.

It is easy, looking back across the centuries, simply to condemn the church (and others involved) for their shortcomings and lack of vision in their provision for the sick, the elderly and the impoverished. From the vantage point of today, workhouses, asylums and almshouses often appear as symbols of the inhumanity, rather than the humanity of a past age, and we find it hard to believe that people should have been condemned to live in what we perceive as such appalling conditions. It is no part of my task here to attempt to defend the church of the past against such criticisms, but merely to note that it was often through the agency of the local parish or incumbent or a particular benefactor that any provision at all (however inadequate it may seem to us) was made for the needy, the outcasts and the elderly. Standards undoubtedly varied, and the best of the almshouses (such as the Whitgift Almshouses in Croydon) would have been extremely comfortable, whilst the worst of the asylums and workhouses must have seemed barely, if at all, more tolerable than nothing at all. The fact remains, however, that the church did attempt to make some provision for the most underprivileged and unfortunate groups within society, and this fact, though it did not contribute directly to the power of the church, nonetheless ensured that the church remained woven into the fabric of society at all levels, and also wielded a good deal of local influence through appointments to posts in such institutions and through its voice in deciding who should and who should not be eligible for the care provided by them.

There was, in addition, running alongside this institutional philanthropy, a good deal of personal and private philanthropy on the part of the clergy. Many of the eighteenth and nineteenth-century clerical diaries and letters record the feeding of beggars, the provision of soup for the poor, extra food for mothers and their young children and the like, and it is unlikely that Parson Woodforde and James Kilvert and their fellow diarists were alone in this local dispensation of charity; often, it must be acknowledged to their credit, amounting to a very substantial contribution out of their own very modest means. Once again, the effects of this, though indirect, are not hard to see. The clergy, and through them the church, acquired a far-reaching moral influence over the lives of their parishioners. It was not that they necessarily sought such influence and authority, but merely that it is, in the nature of things, hard to ignore the claims of someone who has fed or clothed you and your family during a time of crisis or particular need.

Both privately and publicly, then, the church exercised a considerable power over the lives of a substantial percentage of the population, both in practical terms through the provision of benefits (thereby continuing a tradition of church involvement with 'social charity' which originated in the monasteries), and also in spiritual and moral terms as a result of the network of 'indebtedness' which arose from this. Such influence and authority may have been acquired in some cases deliberately and calculatingly, and in others unconsciously and even unwillingly, and it may or may not have been in any sense desirable. These questions of evaluation are not at issue here: what is significant for our purposes is simply that, for better or for worse, the influence of the church was enhanced as a by-product of philanthropy.

With certain variations, this same picture is broadly repeated in the field of education, especially during the nineteenth century. Indeed, education is perhaps the area in which the church has been most, and most effectively, socially active. For centuries indeed, and stretching back to the earliest days of Christianity in England, most education had been in the hands of the church (as it had been throughout the whole of Europe thanks to the monastic intellectual tradition), and it was symptomatic that degrees at Oxford and Cambridge Universities were conferred only on those who were to be ordained into holy orders. Given such a background, it was hardly surprising that the church should have played an active part when it came to the provision of education for the great mass of the population whose education had formerly been almost entirely neglected.

As the nineteenth century progressed, there were fewer and fewer parishes which did not have their own primary school, and likewise many of the major nineteenth-century public school foundations were connected, as also were several of the older mediaeval and Tudor foundations, either directly or indirectly, with the church. The effects of this were two-fold, and differed radically in the short term and the long term. In the short term, the result was, inevitably, to enhance the prestige of the church and to reinforce its place at the very centre of the life of society: it was the provider of learning, secular as well as sacred, and virtually the whole of society came within its orbit for at least a few years of their lives. In the longer term, the effect was, ironically, to reduce drastically the authority of the church as more and more people became better informed, more literate and more able to think for themselves. Unquestioned obedience to any external authority became a thing of the past, and a new and critical intelligence was brought to bear on the very organization which had fostered the growth of that intelligence! Similarly, the 'supremacy' of the church as being the milieu of the better educated was lost, as people educated by that church entered the realms of science, philosophy, history and so on. At least until the turn of the present century, however, it is probably true that its role in the provision of education contributed to, rather than detracted from, the social standing and 'status' of the church.

Socially then, as well as politically, the church of England found itself – and on the whole took good care to keep itself – at the hub of the nation's life. The implications for the authority of the church are less direct in the social sphere than in the political one, but they are equally real.

III

Significant as these political and social factors undoubtedly have been in underpinning the authority of the church, there is one final idea, or cluster of ideas, which though far less discrete and much harder accurately to pin down, has nevertheless exercised a substantial influence on people's vision of the Church of England, both from within itself and in the eyes of the nation at large. This cluster of ideas (or perhaps, more properly, feelings) is centred around the perception of the Anglican Church as being – in much the same manner as cricket – somehow quintessentially 'English'. Indeed, the aptness of the comparison with the 'Englishness' of cricket is readily borne out by the frequency with which the two go together, not least in the fact that the *Church Times* sponsors an inter-diocesan cricket competition!

Such a sense of 'Englishness' is intrinsically something rather nebulous. One cannot say in what precise ways the Church of England is 'English' any more than one can say precisely why Elgar's *Pomp and Circumstance* marches are 'English', but the feeling and the emotive power for many people are the same, and this gentle and genteel patriotic flavour to the church has helped to support its claims whilst even 'Englishness' has been seen as a 'virtue'. Indeed this feeling of identity between the Church of England and what might be called the 'spirit of England' helps to explain the furore and outrage surrounding Bishop Bell of Chichester during the Second World War. It is clear that the sense of having a national church which was an intrinsic part of the national identity was alive and emotive as recently as fifty years ago – and quite possibly would surface again if ever similar circumstances arose in the future.

The other manifestation of this 'spirit of Englishness' which still surrounds the Church of England today is the extent to which people in England would describe themselves (unless, of course, they have any other specific ecclesiastical allegiance) as being 'C of E'. It is true that the percentage of people who would so describe themselves has fallen in the last generation or two, but the number of people who still find it necessary to be baptized, married and buried through the offices of the church, or who subscribe to the so-called 'three times a year' mentality with regard to church attendance, is still remarkable. Even in an increasingly post-Christian society there is still a sense that it is almost automatic and socially 'respectable' to be 'C of E', at least nominally even if not actively. The place of the Church of England and the sense of its innate 'Englishness' is rooted at least as much in people's subconscious, or even pre-conscious, minds as it is in their conscious thought and decision-making.

Although it is necessarily a somewhat vague and unspecific thing, this sense of 'Englishness' is intimately related to the more specific sources of authority outlined earlier in this chapter. That is, it both feeds on, and in turn reinforces the political and social aspects of the church's involvement with the national life. The 'Englishness' of the church is perhaps initially created by this overt involvement, but once created, it then becomes a powerful force which fosters in its turn the furtherance of that sense of identity between nation and church, with predictable consequences for the authority of the church itself.

Intangible it may be, but the extent to which Anglicanism is imbued with this sense of 'Englishness' is reflected in the very name of Anglicanism: the name of the communion is itself a symbol of this quality. And the quality itself is manifestly more than a symbol as a glance at more than one of the Anglican provinces would confirm. By way of an apt – if unlikely – example, I refer to the experience of a group of Kenyan Anglicans who found themselves living for several months in my own parish on the west coast of County Donegal in Ireland. After a few weeks I asked them how they coped with our worship, which I had assumed was likely to be very different and probably less colourful than theirs at home. 'Not at all,' they replied, and explained that they too used the Book of Common Prayer and a largely Victorian hymnal! English colonialism may have died, but its legacy is still to be seen in the thoroughly 'English' worship of at least one group of contemporary black Anglican Christians.

In all of these ways, then, political, social, and more generally in its quintessentially 'English' ethos, the Church of England has long enjoyed a privileged place in English society, and with that place it has enjoyed too a substantial authority within society, the right to exercise which has only relatively recently been seriously questioned, even if it has not always necessarily been obeyed.

2

Structural Authority

I

The historical authority of the church which we have examined in chapter 1 has been largely external in its origins. Forces outside the church itself have combined to impart an authority to the church *vis-a-vis* the society around it. Equally important, however, is the internal authority of the church – in other words the authority by which it governs itself, makes its decisions and conveys its expectations of its members, both lay and clerical. In 1990 G. R. Evans published an excellent study of precisely this issue, and, significantly for the future, her thinking was firmly set within an inter-provincial and an ecumenical context. For her, the decisions, and the decision-making structure of Anglicanism, could no longer be exercised or examined in isolation, but must of necessity be viewed in the light of their ramifications for the wider church catholic. Thus her aim, as expressed in the Preface was that:

> This study tries to provide a working brief on the inter-relationship of the complex of 'authority' questions which confronts the Anglican Communion today, most noticeably in the area of 'provincial autonomy' [a debate greatly fuelled by the piecemeal ordination of women in particular provinces], but on many other fronts too; and to do so in the context of a goal of universality.[1]

Dr Evans' focus (although her historical material is substantial) is largely on the possibilities open to Anglicanism in the future, especially in an ecumenical setting. By contrast to this, the intent of this chapter is simply to outline in brief the ways in which the centuries' old hierarchical authority of the Anglican Church (the survival of which Dr Evans would equally question) has been eroded during a period of not much more than seventy or eighty years.

It has become fashionable in the latter part of our own century to question the need for any kind of fixed structures or 'chains of command' whatsoever, but if one is to be realistic rather than idealistic it would appear from the evidence of human history that every organization of any size requires some sort of authority structure in order to function effectively, and the fact that the church is a religious – and therefore primarily a spiritual – organization does not appear in any way to exempt it from this requirement. On the contrary, the church has always set great store by some kind of hierarchical authority, and the question has been not whether such authority should exist, but exactly how it should be wielded and by whom.

During the Apostolic era it would, admittedly, seem as though this kind of authority did not exist: the Apostles merely exercising a kind of charismatic authority rather than a directly structured authority derived from any office they held. Whether this was always effective or not may well be another matter: it would appear from the New Testament evidence (and especially from the Second Letter to the Corinthians) that St Paul at least occasionally had a traumatic time attempting to discipline or control the communities which he had helped to found! At any rate it did not take many years before this charismatic authority had collapsed (presumably as the first generation of Christian leaders died out) and been superseded by a gradually emerging system of authority with a clearly-defined hierarchical structure. Thus as early as the first decade of the second century, Ignatius could write to the Ephesians: 'Wherefore it is fitting that ye also should run together in accordance with the will of the bishop who by God's appointment rules over you,'[2] and a little later in the same epistle: 'It is manifest, therefore, that we should look upon the bishop even as we would look upon the Lord himself, standing, as he does before the Lord,'[3] and similar passages are to be found in almost every one of the Ignatian epistles. By even this early stage in the church's history, then, the basic outlines of the three-fold order of ministry of bishops, priests and deacons had emerged, and throughout the succeeding centuries this ordering has remained fundamental to the catholic church.

Around this constant central structure, however, there have admittedly been major upheavals and disputes from time to time as to where ultimate authority lies. The centuries of the patristic era are littered with arguments between patriarchs, bishops, councils and synods, and liberally peppered with mutual pronouncements of anathema and excommunication for one reason or another.

Following the conversion of the Emperor Constantine the situation was further complicated by his involvement in church affairs, and it became even more unclear who effectively governed the church – the bishops, the councils, or the Emperor. The awkwardness of the situation is characterized by a letter of Eusebius of Caesarea to his church on the subject of the creed which resulted from the Council of Nicaea. In this letter he is constrained to refer to the Emperor in the most glowing terms as 'our most pious Emperor' and, even more extravagantly as 'our most wise and religious Emperor',[4] even when he is actually unhappy about the outcome of Nicaea (which Constantine had called together) and disagrees with some of its formulations. At this stage in the church's history it was less than clear whether authority lay ultimately with the Council in its purely religious capacity, or with the Emperor as exercising also a temporal authority – and even if authority lay primarily with the Council it was still an authority which had to be exercised in such a way as to avoid incurring the Emperor's overt displeasure.

Certainly the wrangles over power (both within the church and between the church and the state) continued and even intensified at certain periods, most notably around the Great Schism of 1054, but in general the trend towards a recognizably hierarchical system of authority progressed unchecked, and during the Middle Ages the power of the Pope had become such that he could at times hold even the Holy Roman Emperor to account, rather than the other way around – although it must be admitted that the Emperor usually managed to exact his revenge in some way or another on a subsequent occasion! Thus, broadly speaking, from the time of Leo the Great until the Reformation, the church (initially in its entirety, and after 1054 in the West) recognized and exercised a well-defined hierarchical power structure. It may not always have been perfect, but for the most part it was effective: the church was governed on the whole efficiently, even if it was at times governed badly rather than well!

As time went by, also, the overt superstructure of authority – particularly the system of bishops, priests and deacons – became supported by a vast network of Canon Law which functioned as a kind of hidden scaffolding for the hierarchy. It provided codified 'do's' and 'don'ts' for virtually any situation, and a framework within which transgressors could be easily identified and brought to account. Indeed, by the time of the Reformation, the Roman Catholic Church exerted almost total control over the lives of its members, and certainly over its clergy. Looking back from our democratic and enlightened viewpoint, the system may appear to us to have been authoritarian, harsh, and indeed corrupt, but it was most certainly operated with a good deal of competency, if not always of holiness!

Following the Reformation, the Church of England largely reduplicated the earlier Roman Catholic authority structure – indeed it left the vast bulk of it in place, hence its claim to be 'catholic and reformed' rather than 'Protestant' in the sense in which the continental Reformed churches are 'Protestant'. The hierarchy of clerical orders was left untouched, and the only major change in this respect was the denial of supreme power to any one individual. The system became more collegial as far as the bishops were concerned, and this is a development which has only been further ratified and applied during the succeeding centuries. Thus, whilst the primacy of the Archbishop of Canterbury has always been acknowledged, it has become (especially as the Anglican Communion has spread during the last one hundred and fifty years or so) not so much a straightforward primacy of power, but rather a primacy of spiritual and moral standing. Thus he has become not a monarchical figure, but increasingly a *primus inter pares*, which standing, of course, still holds good today throughout the Anglican Communion.

With this exception, however, the arrangements for church government remained as hierarchical as ever they were. Again these arrangements were supported by the vast framework of Canon Law, much of it unchanged in substance after the Reformation, and the overt authority of priests and especially of bishops was reinforced by the continued arrogation of certain roles and functions to them alone. Thus, as still today, the priest alone is authorized to absolve, bless and consecrate the elements at the Holy Communion, and the bishop alone is empowered to confirm and to ordain, and, of course, to consecrate his fellow bishops. The power of the hierarchy in matters sacred was thus absolute, but lest this was not enough to come across with sufficient force to the mass of the population it was then reinforced by the power of the priest and his church in the more secular world of daily life, through the right of the church to receives tithes and Easter offerings as tokens of esteem from a grateful flock!

During the centuries following the Reformation, then, a distinctive pattern of ecclesiastical authority emerged in England, but the hierarchical structures of the Anglican Church have not remained entirely stagnant since the mid-sixteenth century. They have, to an extent at least, adapted, or attempted to adapt, to changing times and needs. Certainly there has been a basic continuity of authority, but Anglicanism, if often marginally sluggish in its response to change, has never been entirely petrified! During times in which society has been large static, so too has been the church, but there have been substantial changes especially during the last one hundred years or so, which accurately reflect the changed social conditions and status of much of the population as a result of such things as the more widespread educational opportunities (often provided by the church itself) which were touched on in chapter 1.

Broadly speaking, a more educated populace which was better able than previously to think for itself and make decisions for itself became, by the latter decades of the nineteenth century, a force to be reckoned with in terms of church government. It is no coincidence that the convening of the Convocations of Canterbury and York dates from this period, as a newly-educated and literate laity began to need (and expect) to be taken into account in the structures of the church. This process, begun in the 1870s, has of course gathered pace ever since as Convocations have developed into synods which now have many wide-ranging and effective executive powers in terms of the policies and decisions of the church. Similarly, the involvement of more people in church government has taken place not merely at national level, but also at a more local level, and there is today a clear framework of deanery and diocesan synods as well as countless boards and committees, all of which guarantee a wide-ranging involvement in the life and government of the church on the part of lay people, as well as of a much larger number of clergy than previously.

This increased authority for lay people – and a genuine authority it most certainly is, as the emergence of a House of Laity has enabled lay people to exercise an influence in matters of church policy and government previously denied to them – has altered the balance of power within the Anglican Communion in that it has set Synods especially alongside bishops, and indeed often effectively over them when it comes to making major changes in church order or finance. (Interestingly, however, the situation has never been entirely resolved as to where 'power' in such issues ought to reside, as may be seen by the recent dispute in Wales concerning the bishops' right or lack of it to re-introduce legislation providing for the ordination of women.) At the same time, the alterations in the status and involvement of lay people have left unchanged the basic day-to-day authority structure of the church, in which the bishop is the spiritual leader in his diocese and in which both lay people and clergy are assumed to be under his authority – albeit an authority of servanthood.

Thus, for example, as far as the clergy are concerned, the provisions of the Ordinal in its recent revisions are left largely unaltered in sense even if not always in language. I refer, for convenience, to the Ordinals of my own province, the Church of Ireland, but though the wording may vary, the basic assumptions and the promises which the service of Ordination demands do not vary greatly from province to province. In the 1662 Ordinal, the candidates for ordination are asked by the Bishop: 'Will you reverently obey your Ordinary, and other chief Ministers, unto whom is committed the charge and government over you, following with a glad mind and will their godly admonitions, and submitting yourselves to their godly judgments?' and they respond: 'I will do so, the Lord being my helper.'[5] The substance of this promise is maintained in the 1993 Revised Ordinal, in which the question reads: 'Will you accept the discipline of this church and give respect to those set over you in the Lord?' and the candidate replies: 'By the help of God, I will.'[6] These general promises of obedience are then reinforced and made more specific by the Declarations which every Incumbent of a parish is required to make at his or her Institution. Thus Articles Five and Six of the Declarations read:

> I will render all due reverence and canonical obedience to M., Archbishop (*or* Bishop) of X., and his successors, Archbishops (*or* Bishops) of X., in all lawful and honest commands.
>
> I promise to submit myself to the authority of the Church of *Ireland*, and to the Laws and Tribunals thereof.[7]

The structures of authority – and the requirement to obey that authority, at least on the part of the clergy – are still, then, very firmly in place. In that sense, nothing has changed significantly during the centuries: the church is still hierarchically ordered, and obedience to that hierarchy is enjoined upon its members. And yet, for all this outward stability, something *has* changed. If the authority structure remains the same, then certainly the attitude of the faithful, both lay and clerical, towards it has for the most part altered radically. It is undoubtedly healthy and entirely constructive that today there is no cringing before the authority of the church, but it is also true – and potentially less beneficial – that increasing numbers of people even within the church feel within their rights to disregard that authority altogether. It remains to be established how this radical change in perspective has come about.

35

II

The several strands of Anglican authority identified here have been isolated and treated in separate chapters merely for the sake of clarity and convenience, but they are all, of course, inextricably linked, each of them having, in any number of ways, fed and fostered each of the others. So, in this instance, the hierarchical and structural authority with which we are concerned here has been, for many centuries, tied in very closely with the historical factors which were outlined in chapter 1. Some of the connections were hinted at there, such as the links between the church and the state through which the hierarchy of the church acquired a reflected authority from the hierarchy of the state, but there are other points of intersection between them also. While it is true, therefore, that sociologists and social historians may have questioned the all-embracingness of social pressure towards conformity in previous generations, there seems little doubt that such pressures did exist, and were substantial, even if not entirely overwhelming. There was, for the most part, an expectation with regard to social conventions and niceties, and these conventions included for many, though not for all, churchgoing, and a broad acceptance of the church as being a necessary part of the fabric of society. Furthermore, there were, as one moves further back in time, also ecclesiastical courts and penalties to enforce obedience upon clergy and laity alike. This social pressure – though not, thankfully, that of the courts – is still a reality in some parts of the world. There are, for example, in Ireland, and especially in the predominantly Roman Catholic rural areas, many men who attend Mass not out of any great personal conviction, but simply because it is easier to do so than to have the 'weemun' of the family 'giving out' for the rest of Sunday about their non-attendance!

For the most part, however, these pressures towards

conformity have weakened both socially and ecclesiastically, and this has affected both peoples' attitudes and their practice in relation to the church. Fewer couples, for example, now marry in church than even a generation or two ago, and fewer of their children are now baptized. These changes in peoples' practice reflect a fundamental shift of attitude in which individuals have become more conscious of their individuality and consequently more able to declare themselves unwilling to 'obey' the dictates of the church, or even to attend it.

The same shift of attitude is present too even among those who remain attached to the church as regular churchgoers. In years gone by James Woodforde could publicly upbraid his congregation for their 'Impudence' in singing rather than saying the responses,[8] and he could expect the Vestry to acquiesce in most of his wishes, and records in his diary that on one occasion in particular, 'They all behaved extremely obliging to their Rector.'[9] A similar primacy was accorded to the church in matters not just of ecclesiastical order, but of social and moral issues also, and a clergyman could expect a sermon on honesty, chastity or social duties to be listened to and taken to heart. In a very real sense the church exercised a certain discipline over the lives of its members. In part this discipline may have been over-paternalistic and contributed towards an attitude of subservience and dependency on the part of lay people, but equally, in part it is not entirely unreasonable for the church to expect certain standards of behaviour and morality among its members.

At the present time, however, this discipline has been largely eroded, and the church can speak on virtually any social or moral issue it likes without necessarily being heeded even by its own members. In an increasingly individualistic society most people have their own notions and standards of what is right or appropriate, and are more willing to listen to their own conscience than to any outside arbiter of morality. The rise of the individual conscience and with it of individual responsibility is in one sense beneficial – it is obviously desirable for people to feel that they are responsible for their own lives and decisions. At the same time, however, there is a very real danger that one's conscience can be lulled to sleep whenever it is likely to prove too inconvenient if there is not some external as well as internal input into one's moral decision-making. Whilst, therefore, one would not regret the demise of authoritarianism on the part of the church, it is arguable that the reaction has gone too far, and that although blind obedience to external authority is not to be encouraged, yet there might still usefully be a place for retaining an external pattern of spiritual and ethical excellence as a corrective to the potential excesses of individualism.

In spite of these changes in recent times, the concept and the structure of hierarchical authority are still in place within the Anglican Communion. In certain other communions, most notably the Roman Catholic Church, this structure and authority are still imbued with a good deal of real power – indeed, as it often appears, too much power. Within Anglicanism, however, this structural hierarchical authority is increasingly an authority in name rather than reality. The scaffolding is still there, but the building behind it appears to have fallen down! In the relatively infrequent instances when the authority is real, it depends more upon the moral stature of a particular individual than it does upon any office which he or she may hold. In the same way, there are virtually no sanctions which can be invoked by the church if that authority is disregarded. The majority – though admittedly not all – of the clergy are still freeholders, and lay people are, effectively, 'volunteers' who are quite entitled to vote with their feet and go elsewhere if they do not approve of what is happening in their own church or do not wish to comply with any or all of its 'demands'.

III

The church's response – by which I mean that of its legislators and bishops – to this situation is at present somewhat uncertain. In itself this is hardly surprising since it is a radically new problem which no previous generation has had to face in the same way before. At the same time, interestingly, this same uncertainty is a further indication of the problem of vanished or diminished authority – the problem of what to do about having no authority does not arise unless one is conscious of having no authority!

It is perhaps in reaction to this dilemma that the Anglican Church has shown an increasing interest in recent years in business methods and management models. There has been much debate, both formally in synods and informally in the correspondence columns of the *Church Times* for example, as to whether the church is justified in adopting the practices of the secular world in this way. Is the church 'set apart' in such a way as to make business methods inappropriate, or is it sufficiently similar in organizational structure to benefit from their introduction? Are 'management' and account-ability incompatible with the concept of vocation and with the somewhat intangible nature of the clergyman's role? Or is it high time that the clergy stopped claiming to be different in kind from other employees of large organizations and accepted their position as both managers themselves and employees who are managed by others?

One of the most reflective and thought-provoking discussions of this issue to appear recently was that by Ian R. Boyd in *Theology*. He examines in some detail why the 'management model' has become so prevalent in the church today, and he identifies as the prime reason for this the fact that the church has somewhat lost its theological bearings especially as far as the nature and the tasks of the full-time ministry are concerned, and therefore 'management theory' has been drafted in to fill the resulting theological vacuum. In essence this idea is complimentary to my own remarks above, that interest in management has increased as authority and distinctive ecclesiological identity have declined. Such a development may be understandable, but it brings with it substantial (and subtle) dangers both for the present and for the future of the church:

> ...[bureaucratic rationality] is the only form of rationality which can flourish [in a church which espouses it]...In particular, it cannot recognize any claim to rationality in the choice of the ends of the organization. This is very worrying indeed. For it implies that as the Church and its clergy conform to the managerial model, they can no longer recognize any theological reasoning about the purpose or aims of the Church. Like a young cuckoo, bureaucratic rationality is not content just to have a place in the nest: it must surreptitiously remove the theological eggs until it has no rivals. Bureaucratic rationality subverts the ends of an organization where that organization seeks to reflect rationally on its own nature, language and action. Perhaps this is the reason for the oft-lamented drop in the level of theological literacy and activity among parish clergy: it is not just pressure of other duties – rather there is a serious conflict between the role of 'religious organizer' and the ability to engage in meaningful reflection on the language and action of the Church. To try to do both is to attempt to straddle two competing rationalities. It is an attempt which often proves painful.[10]

Whether or not Ian Boyd is accurate in his warning of the dangers implicit in 'bureaucratic rationality' (although I, for one, suspect that he may well be correct), it does seem evident that this new-found interest in the world of management methods is a reflection of, and a reaction to, a lack of self-confidence on the part of the church in its traditional understanding of itself, its identity and its authority.

In spite of this timely warning from Ian Boyd, though, it appears that this debate will rumble on for some time yet, and will, in all probability, never be entirely resolved, since there is a valid case to be made (in moderation at least) for the church's similarity as well as its dissimilarity to other large organizations. In the meantime, and with many local variations of emphasis and intensity, the church is beginning to adopt at least some of the managerial methods and skills from the world of business. Clergy are now sent on courses (beginning as early as their post-ordination training course, or even their days at theological college) to learn how to conduct meetings, motivate other people, work with small groups, solve problems and deal constructively with angry people or situations of conflict. Likewise most of the English dioceses (as well as those in America and a growing number in Ireland) have introduced one form or another of clergy appraisal or review. In some this is done on a peer basis, in others it is arranged hierarchically, but in either case it is nonetheless a move towards a more effective management of the clergy themselves, together with at least some emphasis on accountability in a clergyman's work.

That this interest in business management methods should have surfaced at this particular point in time is not, I believe, a coincidence. It would appear to represent an effort to provide an alternative authority structure to the straightforwardly hierarchical one which has been in operation for so long. The kind of authority structure which is being imparted is one which does not rest solely upon 'power' or vertical institutional authority, but one which also utilizes particular skills and training. Perhaps the unspoken hope is that the clergy in particular will respond favourably to the idea that their immediate seniors have been trained in an appropriate way for their positions, and that there will arise as a result a feeling more of 'management' than of simple 'authority'. In the past such a change of emphasis was not needed, and the fact that it is happening in our own age is a good index of the decline in credibility of the old overtly hierarchical system.

Furthermore, the same reasoning holds good not just within the ranks of the clergy themselves, but also in the parochial relationships between clergy and lay people. No longer are the clergy able to invoke the authority of their office, and they are finding increasingly that it is more effective to learn how to 'manage' people than it is to attempt to coerce them by behaving in an authoritarian manner. It would appear that the church, albeit in a largely unspoken fashion, is in the process of recognizing its own authority crisis and of making the first tentative steps towards responding to it, although it is to be hoped that as this process continues the church will heed the dangers of an over-emphasis on 'bureaucratic rationality' referred to above. Managerial skills may well be a useful tool for the future, but this must not be at the expense of seeing the church's remaining 'theological eggs' pushed out of the nest!

An additional factor in the response of the church during the next decade or two to its current crisis of authority will be the consequences of the recent decisions to ordain women within various of the provinces of the Anglican Communion. The measure may not have been designed to contribute to the issue of authority, but it will almost undoubtedly have a complicating effect on it, however unintentional it may be. It is too early yet to make concrete predictions, but it will at least be interesting to see how the presence of growing numbers of female clergy affects the church's attitude to authority. Traditionally the authority exercised by the clergy has been paternalistic – indeed often authoritarian – and, for the most part at least, this would seem to be a masculine style of leadership. One hesitates to generalize on such matters, but on the whole women may well turn out to favour a more collaborative style of ministry, both among clergy and between clergy and lay people, and in the fullness of time this may itself contribute towards further changes in the church's understanding of itself and of its authority. In the shorter-term, though, whilst the church gets used to the presence of women clergy and resolves the various issues surrounding their ordination, their presence will, unfortunately, simply further complicate the church's attitude to authority and leave it even more unclear exactly where authority can be said to reside. There would appear to be at least three separate issues of authority which their ordination has raised: first, a question surrounding the authority of those who ordained them – did they, in fact, have the authority (rather than merely the power) to do so; secondly, the challenge to this authority by those who object to the ordination of women and refuse to submit to the ruling of the church and its synods; and thirdly, the question of the exact status of the authority of the ordained women themselves when this authority (and with it their 'right' to preside at certain liturgical functions such as the eucharist) is plainly not accepted by all.

We shall return to consider these issues more fully in chapter 4. At the present time though, the situation is one in which, for all these nascent changes, the authority structures of the Anglican Church remain in place. It is however, at a turning point. In the past the authority wielded by the hierarchy was a very real one; today this authority is in dispute; and tomorrow, one suspects, the authority attached to office may well decline still further. That the Anglican Church is balanced at the fulcrum at the moment is perfectly characterized by a recent controversy in which authority has been central – that is, the furore surrounding the publication of Anthony Freeman's book, *God in Us*.[11] As a consequence of its publication, Mr Freeman found himself relieved by his bishop first of his diocesan responsibilities, and then some months later of his licence to officiate in his parish also. Regardless of the rights and wrongs involved, which are not at issue in this context, here, apparently, is an example of a hierarchical system working with remarkable efficiency. His bishop, in this case the Bishop of Chichester, possessed enough *real* authority – in terms of his ability to impose sanctions such as the withdrawal of licences – to make this happen. But what is more interesting, although not of much direct help to the unfortunate Mr Freeman, is the instant outcry when the bishop invoked his authority and took this particular course of action. In practice he may still be able to exercise such a degree of authority – although with any clergyman who was an Incumbent and therefore a freeholder his authority would be far more limited – but there is a major question around in the minds of many people, not all of whom would necessarily agree with Mr Freeman doctrinally, as to whether any bishop *should* be empowered to act in this way. In this particular instance, just as we have argued is the case in more general terms, the structures of direct authority are still in place, but attitudes towards them are changing radically. A few generations ago almost no one would have questioned a bishop's right to discipline his clergy. The fact that such a public controversy can arise as it has in this case is a measure of how dramatically attitudes towards authority have changed. It may very well be only a matter of time before the practice of the church must change also.

3

Biblical and Doctrinal Authority

I

A revealing starting point, in that it reinforces once again the multifarious points of contact between the various kinds of authority which we are considering, is the Anthony Freeman 'affair' with which we concluded the previous chapter. The controversy surrounding his dismissal had its origins in the non-realist theology which he propounded in his book *God in Us*. What was – and is – essentially at issue is the degree of latitude which should be allowed, doctrinally speaking, to those who speak and write in the name of the church. In writing *God in Us* Anthony Freeman has overtly challenged the traditional doctrinal and credal basis of Anglican Christianity. Along with other thinkers – most particularly Don Cupitt and David A. Hart – he has opened up the question of what are, or should be, the limits of belief. The radical nature of this challenge is highlighted by the titles of several of the books involved, Don Cupitt's *Taking Leave of God* and David A. Hart's *Faith in Doubt* being prime examples.[1]

Again, in this context, the fact that any sort of debate – let alone such a furore as has surrounded *God in Us* – could take place is instructive. Authority is being challenged on not one, but two counts. In the previous chapter we focussed on the challenge to the hierarchy as to whether it should be in a position to wield the kind of authority which Bishop Kemp has 'enjoyed' – if that is the right word! – in this case; but it is equally clear that there is a similar challenge to the church's 'right' to define the limits of belief. Thus, for example, writing in even the relatively conservative atmosphere of *The Church of Ireland Gazette* Tim Peacock could voice the opinion that:

> I confess that I was surprised to learn that one year before he lost his parish he was dismissed from a teaching post in the diocese. However unorthodox a teacher's views may be, it is not his job to tell his pupils what to think so much as to teach them to think for themselves and to appreciate the importance of honest thought. I know from experience that some very unorthodox theologians have proved to be stimulating teachers, and often their pupils have little idea of what their teachers in fact believe or disbelieve. The vital consideration is that they are taught to think for themselves.[2]

Whether Anthony Freeman's 'sacking' was appropriate or not is not of prime importance here. What is significant, however, is the degree of support which he and other radical thinkers have found – and not merely among the clergy. Doctrinal libertarianism (or perhaps minimalism would be a more accurate description), is becoming a force to be reckoned with, and it is clear that the credal and doctrinal aspects of faith are, for many, open to criticism and revision in a way that would until recently have been unthinkable.

These credal and doctrinal structures are, however, outwardly at least, still firmly in place, and they are reinforced at a variety of points in the life of the believer. The most obvious such moments are encapsulated in the promises made at baptism and then again at confirmation.

On each occasion the candidates (or in the case of infant baptism, their sponsors) are required to profess their personal allegiance to Christ, their acceptance of the various articles of the Creed, and their intention to orientate their life in a particular way. The promises made are doctrinally specific, especially with regard to the Creed, and the fact that many churches also have a regular service of reaffirmation of baptismal vows suggests that the making of these promises is still seen as meaningful and valuable – although it is likely that this is at least as often for reasons of security and a sense of belonging as it is by virtue of a complete acceptance of all the precise doctrinal implications on the part of the candidate.

The promises made in baptism and confirmation are common to all Christian people, but not surprisingly the church requires further and more explicit promises of those who are to be ordained, and as with the promise of obedience, the content of these doctrinal assents has changed little in over three hundred years. In the 1662 Ordinal the candidate is questioned regarding the authority of scripture:

> Are you persuaded that the holy Scriptures contain sufficiently all doctrine required of necessity for eternal salvation through faith in Jesus Christ? And are you determined out of the said Scriptures to instruct the people committed to your charge; and to teach nothing as required of necessity to eternal salvation, but that which you shall be persuaded may be concluded and proved by the Scripture?[3]

In the 1993 Ordinal, one question has become two, and the authority of the church is set alongside the authority of scripture:

Do you believe and accept the Holy Scriptures as revealing all things necessary for eternal salvation through faith in Jesus Christ?

Do you believe and accept the doctrine of the Christian faith as the Church of Ireland has received it?[4]

Again, as with the promise of obedience, these promises with regard to scripture and the church are made more specific in the service of Institution. Article Two of the Declarations reads:

I assent to the Thirty-nine Articles of Religion, and to the Book of Common Prayer, and of the Ordering of Bishops, Priests and Deacons. I believe the doctrine of the Church of *Ireland*, as therein set forth, to be agreeable to the Word of God; and in Public Prayer and Administration of the Sacraments I will use the form in the said Book prescribed, and none other, except so far as shall be allowed by the lawful authority of the Church.[5]

The scriptures and the church as their interpreter are once more set side by side, allegiance to both is explicitly declared. Anglicanism may not have a founding doctrinal and ecclesiological charter such as the Westminster Confession, for example, but it nonetheless requires both of its lay people and especially of its clergy, an acknowledgment of the authority of scripture and of the place of doctrine in the spiritual life of the believer.

This apparently high estimation of both scripture and doctrine is then reinforced week by week in the public worship of the church, including as it does either two or three readings from scripture, as well as psalms and scriptural canticles, and the recital of either the Apostles Creed or the Nicene Creed at virtually every service. To all outward appearances the traditional order and authority are still functioning, but there is little doubt that for increasing numbers of people they are becoming ever more eviscerated of genuine meaning. The words are still said, but the perceptions and attitudes with which people approach them have changed and are continuing to change. Don Cupitt and Anthony Freeman may be operating at the sharp end of radicalism, but their views would find at least an echo in the intellectual explorations and spiritual experiences of many intelligent lay people also. It may well be that the radicals have over-stated their case, and that few people would be willing to go along with their out-and-out anti-realism, but they have correctly divined that there is a widespread unease about just how the ancient formulations of faith can still be validly upheld in the late twentieth century. It remains to be seen how that unease originated and why it has steadily gained ground since then.

II

Until approximately one hundred and fifty years ago – taking Strauss' *Das Leben Jesu* as a turning point – faith was what might be termed 'pre-critical'. This term is in no sense derogatory. It does not deny the wisdom and rich spiritual insight of thinkers, preachers and writers from the New Testament onwards, and it does not imply that the faith of previous ages was simplistic or naive. Thus there is also no connection between this pre-critical faith and present-day fundamentalism which is an attempt to deny not only the modern critical consciousness but which would also repudiate the allegorical and typological interpretations of scripture favoured by a number of patristic writers. Fundamentalism is not 'pre-critical', but anti-critical and anti-intellectual, and therefore stands in opposition to the intellectual searches and speculations of any age, and not merely the present one.

So what is meant here by the term 'pre-critical'? Principally, the term defines the intellectual world before the advent of modern self-consciousness and self-reflexiveness and the consequent growing scepticism with regard to empirical knowledge and the nature of both matter and spirit. In terms of philosophy and intellectual endeavour generally the crucial period is that of the mid to late eighteenth century, the so-called 'Age of Enlightenment', although it took theology (as usual!) a little while to catch up, and it was not until the publication of Strauss' book in 1835 that this new climate of thought seriously began to be reflected in the work of theologians, exegetes and apologists. So the term 'pre-critical' is only intended to suggest that the faith and thought of previous ages were simply those of their time, and therefore bounded by the limits of contemporary scientific and epistemological understanding.

In this thought-world the ancient categories of Christian doctrine could continue to exist and be found readily meaningful, and the pages of scripture could still be read (though again it must be stressed, not necessarily in a fundamentalist fashion) as a reliable and inspired account of God's dealings with the human race. God was indeed in his heaven, and all, therefore, was right with the world.

Into this apparently stable and peaceful atmosphere erupted, during the early years of the nineteenth century, the fall-out from the previous two centuries of thought from Hume and Descartes to Hegel and Kant – and rationalism and, increasingly, scepticism became the order of the day.

Initially the effects of this were felt largely in terms of the understanding of scripture in general, and the reliability of the Gospels in particular as an accurate record of the life of Jesus – a reliability which had almost vanished by the end of the century even in the eyes of so devout and pious a thinker as Albert Schweitzer, whose *Quest for the Historical Jesus* ended, essentially, only in unresolved questions.

Alongside this growing sense of uncertainty concerning the historical verisimilitude of scripture, a great multiplicity of forces combined as the nineteenth century advanced to put an intense pressure on the traditional categories of faith and interpretations of scripture. A growing sense of historical and literary criticism resulted in new analyses of the biblical writings, and the biblical critics assigned their texts more and more to the realm of literature than to that of divinely inspired dictation. Simultaneously the ever more rapid strides in scientific discovery forced theologians, albeit often reluctantly, to re-assess the biblical texts in the context of that new knowledge. The origins of the universe stretched ever further backwards into time; evolution appeared to conflict with the idea of divine creation; and the human race found itself at once more fascinating as an object of scientific study, and yet less significant as a result of the revelation of the hitherto unimagined immensity of cosmic space and time.

For many thoughtful mid-Victorians the result of this intellectual ferment was a disturbed and unsettled faith – or indeed increasingly as time progressed, no faith at all. Matthew Arnold's celebrated poem 'Dover Beach' is only one particularly evocative manifestation of this unease, and the correspondence and diaries of a host of other Victorians, both eminent and otherwise, reveal precisely the same tensions and nostalgic longing for a fast-vanishing age of religious certainty. Indeed, even one of the main contributors to the process of secularization, Charles Darwin, could record in his autobiography that: 'I was very unwilling to give up my belief,'[6] and speaks (for all his conviction that belief in God is outdated) with regret of the beauty of a faith which is, somewhat sadly, no longer viable.

51

During the twentieth century Christianity has found itself still further discomfited, as the critical and sceptical spirit of the nineteenth century has gathered ever greater momentum. Two developments in particular would seem to have contributed to the further undermining of religious certainty – relativism and projection theory.

Relativism is not confined to the religious realm, and virtually every discipline has found itself challenged by some form or another of ultimate epistemological scepticism – which is, in effect, what relativism amounts to. In the religious realm, as indeed in others, relativism has its origins in a growing awareness of history, and particularly of human achievements as products of a particular historical era, governed by the constraints and prevailing culture and knowledge of that era. Thus, for example, Mozart's music – for all its charismatic and individual genius – is unmistakably a product of the eighteenth century rather than of the fourteenth century or the twentieth century: it is, in that sense, a product of its time. In itself this historical awareness is epistemologically neutral, but it is only a short step from here to relativism. Once you have established that all human activity is circumscribed by time, place and history in this way, then it is a logical development to suggest that there never has been, and can never be, any age or perspective which has a privileged viewpoint: in other words, just as artefacts and so on are products of their time, so too is knowledge. It is never 'final' or ultimate knowledge, and it is therefore always relative – hence the term 'relativism'.

The consequences for Christianity are obvious and far-reaching if this doctrine is once accepted. For centuries Christians had believed – indeed, one might almost say 'known' – that the revelation of God in scripture was divinely inspired and 'true' in a final sense. It applied to all ages and all places, and as the quotations from the Ordinal referred to above make plain, all the church then had to do was to read off from this revelation those things which were 'essential to salvation' and to see that they were faithfully taught and handed on intact to future generations. Now, suddenly, it seemed that all this certainty was illusory. No more than any other product of human art or knowledge could the Bible claim an ultimate or privileged viewpoint. The various books of scripture were, like any books, simply products of the human mind and imagination, and open to the same standards of judgment and criticism. And, even more importantly, they were – again like any other artefacts – products of their own time and place. Thus the fact that they spoke in certain ways about God's nature and activity did not mean that any other generation had to think in this way. Certainly the books of scripture may bear valuable witness to the religious perceptions and insights of a previous age, and some of them may still be of value to later generations, but they are not 'final' or ultimately 'true' in such a way as to be binding to those who come after. The witness of scripture is not thereby invalidated, but it is effectively deprived of what had previously seemed to be its intrinsic and unshakeable authority.

If relativism has undermined the claims of scripture, then projection theory has gone even further, and offered a formidable challenge to our whole understanding of religion and the spiritual experience of the human race. The progenitor of projection theory in its modern form was the great nineteenth-century German thinker, Ludwig Feuerbach. His ideas are at once most fully and most cogently expressed in his book *The Essence of Christianity*, and the thesis expounded there is, whilst simple in its outlines, yet profound in its implications. For Feuerbach, religion, and in particular the Christian religion, is simply the projection outward of humanity's best qualities. All that is good is thus projected, reified and deified, and all that is worst is kept earth-bound and acknowledged as human. The effect of this is to bind humanity in a servile relationship with a false God, and to divide the individual against himself by denying his access to his own goodness – since now, by definition, all goodness belongs to God. Religion is therefore at once false and destructive of humanity's true potential. For that reason it should be swept away, and the human race should be enabled to rejoice in its own new-found freedom, creativity and goodness and should find, at last, that the God which it had previously worshipped from afar is in fact located nowhere else than within the human heart and spirit.

From these beginnings, the idea of religion as projection has flourished in a colourful diversity of ways. It has been adopted by psychologists, sociologists, political commentators and historians, and its basic premises have been moulded to different purposes by thinkers as diverse as Marx, Freud and Durkheim. There is, it seems, no end to the uses to which the theory of projection may be put. This is, of course, at once its strength and its greatest weakness, for it means that nothing is safe from it, but also that its potential application is so widespread as to deprive it of much of its force: it is a little like the aristocracy in *Iolanthe*: 'When everyone is somebody/Then no one's anybody'! Indeed, it has been pointed out that even Freud's ideas on religion as projection and illusion can be themselves categorized as projection![7] In spite of this, though, projection theory and with it the various other manifestations of relativism have combined in the late nineteenth century and early twentieth century seriously to unsettle the faith of many people, and have significantly contributed to a decline in the perceived authority of the church's scriptural and doctrinal claims.

During the second half of the present century at least, this decline has been further exacerbated by the extent to which

Christianity has increasingly internalized these and other similar movements in contemporary thought. Indeed, very often it has been theologians just as much as philosophers, scientists or sociologists who have been instrumental in offering us a radically new vision of ourselves and our environment. Within the last generation or two, therefore, at least two distinct (although admittedly related) attempts have been made to construct a theology appropriate to our changed, and still changing, epistemological climate. In America the 'death of God' theologians such as Paul Altizer and Mark Taylor have developed what has been called an 'a/theology', whilst in England Don Cupitt (and more recently others also) have explored what Christianity might look like in what has come to be called a 'post-modern' world. Of the two efforts, it is this latter one which appears to me to be in the long term the more significant and fruitful. The principal reason for this is that thinkers such as Cupitt, Anthony Freeman and David A. Hart have not merely reacted to twentieth-century thought by 'abandoning ship' as it were (as some American thinkers have tended to do), but have endeavoured to find a way of reinvigorating, or at least recycling the traditional language of Christianity such that it can be meaningfully employed in a radically new context.

One of the central concerns of this undertaking has been, of course, our understanding of God himself. In a world of relativism and projection the question arises: what value can meaningfully be assigned to the idea of God? An alternative to pronouncing him to be dead is to translate him on to another level of existence, and it is this path which has, on the whole, been taken by the English radical theologians with whom we are concerned here. In their thinking God has moved from being real to being ideal – the sum total of our values, hopes and aspirations. From this fundamental shift of perspective stem all the further developments of thinkers such as Cupitt.[8] Such a vision of God is evidently readily compatible with both the projectionist and relativist positions previously enumerated. In essence, indeed, it is itself a projectionist standpoint, even if in this instance the projection is on to an ideal *within* the human spirit rather than on to a God 'out there'. Similarly, it is a position which accepts as a truism the notion that our values are relative: and therefore to suggest that our ideas of God are equally relative does no harm at all to a radical understanding of God – for God will always be the sum total of our ideals and values whatever they may happen to be at any particular time, and therefore God himself remains, like these values, endlessly open to revision and revaluation. This is not the place for a lengthy discussion of these views, but rather the mere fact that such views can be not only expressed but also espoused by a substantial number of people within the church has major implications for the church's own understanding of its teaching authority – to say nothing of the perception of this authority on the part of those outside the church. In a climate of growing theological radicalism, it appears less and less obvious how the church can convincingly maintain any coherent understanding of its own scriptural, credal or doctrinal authority. Indeed, if scripture, creeds and doctrines are found to be relativistic through and through, then where can such authority any longer be convincingly located? The rock has gone, and shifting sand alone remains.

III

Clearly the main focus of this study is the Anglican communion, but the same questions concerning doctrinal authority can be asked, potentially at least, of every other ecclesial community also – post-modernism, projection and relativism can hardly be assumed to be specifically targeted at Anglicanism! In the face of this challenge how is it that a number of other traditions and denominations are able to continue to claim for themselves a measure of doctrinal and credal authority? Why is it that Anglicanism appears to be uniquely vulnerable to the corrosive spirit of relativism whilst other communities of faith apparently continue to flourish?

The answer to this question lies, I believe, in the particular responses which these other communities have been able to make to radicalism, responses which are no longer available with any real integrity within Anglicanism. First then, and less significant, are the many broadly fundamentalist groups and sects, whose method of response to this – or any other challenge – is at once simple and simplistic, uncompromising and unthinking. It is a response which reveals the ultimate intellectual barrenness of fundamentalism whilst ironically (and sadly) also explaining at least one of the reasons for the 'success' of such groups in the present climate.

Fundamentalism has at least the merit of simplicity, and what could be simpler than to deny the truth or the credibility of something on the grounds that it does not appear in the pages of scripture or threatens to contradict what is written there? And if, as your primary axiom you hold that scripture is in every point the inspired Word of God then this seems, no doubt, a perfectly reasonable course of action. Such, in essence, is the response of fundamentalism to any external threat to the authority of scripture. Anything threatening to, or contradictory to scripture can immediately be ruled out of court on precisely those grounds – that it is contradictory to scripture. This is certainly a convenient response, but the intellectual vacuity of it is hard to credit, and it is easy to see why this is not a viable option for the vast bulk of Anglicans – who would, of course, claim some place for reason in their assessment of faith. Apart from any further failings it rests on one supreme illogicality: the Bible is claimed to be the infallible Word of God simply because it itself claims to be divinely inspired – in other words, because it says in scripture 'God said...' we can therefore be certain that he did indeed speak, and said exactly what he is recorded as saying. However, God has 'said' an equal number of things in the Koran, the Book of Mormon, and countless other sacred texts, and where is the warrant for rating the internal claim for the divine inspiration of Christian scripture any more highly than the same internal claims of any other religious text? Quite simply there is none, and there can be none; and the only 'reason' which can be given is that the believer has made a purely personal and *a priori* assumption that his or her scriptures are the true ones and that therefore the claims which they make to truth are themselves true. The whole argument is self-reflexive to the point of absurdity!

The ludicrousness of such an approach may be readily apparent to anyone who is not already committed to it, but its appeal lies precisely in the fact that it plays the relativists at their own game – it merely reverses each and every one of the arguments employed by the relativists themselves. Where relativism threatens the authority of scripture on external grounds, so in return fundamentalism denies the right of relativism (or any other 'ism') to do any such thing! Neither party can ever realistically hope to convince the other, and the two sides seem condemned to an eternity of mutual antagonism and incomprehension.

However, in spite of its failure to make any significant impression on the relativists' arguments, fundamentalism has nonetheless proved to be remarkably 'successful' in recent years, and it is, on the whole, the extreme fundamentalist churches which are experiencing the most rapid growth at present. Again, the reason is not hard to seek. In a climate of questioning, doubt and re-evaluation many people are crying out for 'certainty', and it is this which fundamentalism claims to be able to provide. Certainly it demands the suspension of one's intellectual faculties, but this is a price which many are willing to pay for the privilege of returning to what had seemed to be a vanished world of security. Indeed, it may well be that the strength of fundamentalism is in direct proportion to the strength of more radical trends, and that the growth of fundamentalism today is an accurate index of the extent to which the trends outlined here have indeed succeeded in undermining the belief structure and authority claims of any more moderate approach to faith. Fundamentalism may leave much to be desired, but it has proved itself to be – for the time being at least – able to resist the challenge of radicalism, and indeed to flourish in the face of it.

Secondly, and of more widespread significance – for one suspects that fundamentalism will one day wither and die as its communal brain finally atrophies beyond the point of no return – is the response of the Roman Catholic Church to the twentieth-century crisis of faith. This response is far more complex than that of fundamentalism, and it may perhaps be accurately characterized as occurring on two levels simultaneously, levels which then inter-react to produce both now and for the future an almost infinite range of possibilities for the church.

On the one hand, therefore, there is the formal response of the *magisterium* of the church – the Pope himself and the various Vatican 'Congregations'. This response has traditionally been a uniformly conservative one, and it would be broadly encompassed in the notion that modern scholarship is in principle acceptable provided that it is always subject to the overriding *magisterium* of the church – exercised through the medium of the *Imprimatur* and the *Nihil Obstat*. Thus the freedom of the individual thinker is at once upheld (in theory at least) whilst in practice being severely curtailed, and indeed many eminent theologians (including several in our own time) have found themselves proscribed for transgressing the acceptable limits of scholarship and intellectual speculation. Curiously this attitude of the *magisterium* is not dissimilar in kind to that of the fundamentalists – it is merely based on an appeal to the church's tradition and dogmatic infallibility rather than on an appeal to scripture as the final arbiter. Such an approach has both its strengths and its weaknesses. Certainly it has been a powerful force in keeping the Roman Catholic Church in being throughout the centuries and giving it a stable (indeed a monolithic) identity, but at the same time it has ensured that that church has changed little during those centuries and is therefore in danger today of looking like a pre-historic relic left over from a past age.

However, this magisterial response is by no means the whole story, for on the other hand there stands the substantial number of theologians who have attempted to approach the various challenges to the church creatively and to find some means of reconciling the traditional categories of the faith and practice of the church with the intellectual atmosphere of the world around them. Their work has often been carried out under threat of proscription – not because they have capitulated to the intellectual climate of their time, but merely because they have acknowledged its existence and attempted to enter into debate with it. It is this attitude of independence of mind (which is yet exercised within the framework of the church) which has led the Roman Catholic Church to produce (and all too often then to disown) some of the most outstanding theologians of our time such as Hans Küng, Edward Schillebeeckx and Pierre Teilhard de Chardin – theologians who may one day be seen as having been in large measure the salvation of the church which disowned them. It is their efforts which are keeping the Roman Catholic Church in touch with the thought worlds of modern philosophy and science, and it may be that in the future the Roman Catholic Church will find a means of reconciling their independence of mind with the church's more conservative *magisterium*. At present the response of the Roman Catholic Church to post-modernism and radicalism looks somewhat schizophrenic, but if in the future there can be some accommodation reached between the church's conservative guardians of the faith and its more creative theologians and apologists then the Roman Catholic Church as a whole (rather than merely isolated figures within it) could again become a valuable presence in the philosophical and theological landscape. In the meantime, the response of the Roman Catholic Church to any challenges will continue to be at once monolithic and schizophrenic!

As far as Anglicanism is concerned, it is in a more difficult position than either fundamentalism or Roman Catholicism. Anglicanism is a theologically finely balanced standpoint, and it can identify neither with the scriptural absolutism of fundamentalism nor with the traditionalist absolutism of the Roman Catholic *magisterium*. More specifically, it has always identified the three fundamental sources of its teaching as being scripture, tradition and reason, and it is hard to counter the claim that modern radical theologians are working from within a tradition, and merely applying the results of contemporary reasoning to our ancient scriptural faith. To appeal to the supreme authority of scripture in such a case is to upset the balance somewhat, and without doing so it is difficult to refute the radicals' argument that if reason causes us to overturn our long-held estimate of scripture then, in the last resort, so be it.

In addition to this, Anglicanism has long prided itself on its tradition of moderation and toleration in matters theological and doctrinal, and this moderation once more plays into the hands of almost anyone who wishes to challenge any aspect of the traditional understanding of faith. Just how problematical this concept of moderation can be is ably illustrated by Stephen Sykes. He discusses the 'deconfessionalization' of Anglicanism during the nineteenth and twentieth centuries, and cites the resulting 'shibboleth that "Anglicans have no special doctrines of their own"', and then comments that for a church which prides itself on holding to the faith of undivided Christendom of the first five centuries:

> It was a serious matter, therefore, when two leading Anglican patristic scholars, Maurice Wiles and Geoffrey Lampe, Regius Professors in both Oxford and Cambridge, publicly argued against trinitarian incarnationalism. What then did Anglicans believe? Were there no limits to Anglican toleration? Was the long-honoured tradition of comprehensiveness now to include a 'liberalism', 'modernism' or 'radicalism' (the labels were various and imprecise) which denied or held in doubt the doctrines of the Trinity and incarnation, and even of the classical doctrine of God? Suddenly, at a moment when the central Anglican tradition ought to have been celebrating its ecumenical and international coming of age, it was plunged into an anxious and self-absorbed debate about its own identity.[9]

Thus Anglicanism faces the problem that if it is to uphold its much valued liberal and tolerant attitude, it can hardly invoke any sanctions against any viewpoint, however destructive or critical, and it is, as a result, almost incumbent upon it (even at the risk of its own demise) to allow even its freest thinkers to roam unchecked.

Anglicanism, therefore, is arguably intrinsically more overtly hard-pressed by radicalism than either fundamenta-

lism or the more monarchical structures of Roman
Catholicism, and it is faced with a dual problem – it needs to
try to find a way to bridge not only the gap which is rapidly
opening up between out-and-out radicals and the more
conservative bulk of believers, but also and more
significantly, the gap which is equally opening up within the
spiritual experience of the ordinary believer who recites an
ancient creed and hears ancient scriptures whilst attempting
at the same time to live in the modern world in which 'faith'
is fast becoming a foreign language. The gap is one which
concerns not merely theology (although that is real enough)
but which also has implications for the daily spiritual practice
of Christians. By way of illustration a prime example might
be that of the language and content of prayer. If a
contemporary Christian reads the occasional prayers in the
Book of Common Prayer he or she will come across prayers
(amongst others) for fine weather, for rain, and for
deliverance from plague. How is that believer to interpret
these and other similar prayers today, for they speak of a
concept of God and his mode of activity which is long since
outmoded? Similarly, when we pray for the nation or for the
sick our prayers are most usually couched in the form of
asking God directly to *do* something, in a way which suggests
a thoroughly interventionist understanding of God's activity
in the world. And so once again the question arises: how can
we square our contemporary understanding of God with the
mediaeval way in which our common worship (and through
it much of our private prayer too) still requires us to address
him? Can we still believe that God acts in the autocratic and
interventionist way which our prayers seem to suggest and to
require of him? And if, as I believe, the answer to this
question is 'No', then we are faced with a yawning gap
between what we say and what we actually believe. Prayer,
and with it the whole life of the church, is thereby placed in
grave danger of becoming one of two things: either a blessed

retreat from reality into a world of childhood security, or else a virtual irrelevance as being something which no longer has any intrinsic connection with the way things actually are in the real world in which we live.

IV

It is abundantly clear, then, that both theologically and practically there is a real problem arising as far as the status of doctrines and creeds (and with them our whole understanding of God and his activity) is concerned, and equally it is clear that exactly how (and how successfully) mainstream Anglicanism tackles the closing of this credibility gap will in all probability make or break our church during the next generation or two. At present the only substantial efforts to fill this gap are those which are being made by more radical thinkers, and their characteristic mode of doing this is to deny the existence of the gap by arguing that scripture, creeds and doctrines are only regulative and not prescriptive, human and not divine, and that therefore the real locus of spiritual endeavour must always be simply the real human world in which we find ourselves. The 'divine' attributes of the church and our faith can be sacrificed in order to preserve a humanistic religious approach to life.

To many people this may sound an attractive option, but as I have argued in detail elsewhere, it is one which is, in the last analysis, spiritually bankrupt. The problem of the credibility gap may be resolved by the removal of the need for creeds and dogma, but nothing of any substance is then invoked in their place. The church may still in theory 'have a gospel to proclaim', but the gospel of thoroughgoing radical Christianity is in danger of becoming so attenuated as to be both meaningless and ineffective.

The danger with issuing such a challenge to radicalism and denying its final validity is that it can look like (or at least be interpreted by radicals as being) a call for a return to biblical fundamentalism. Such, as I have made plain already, is far from being the case here. However, it is vital for theologians to bridge the credibility gap between the categories of a first-century (or even a seventeenth-century) faith and the modern world, whilst yet staying true to the insights of that ancient faith. It will not be easy, but I do not believe that the alternatives left to us are merely those of fundamentalism or radicalism, and it may well turn out to be the case that until and unless a theology is forged which manages to avoid both extremes whilst making an ancient creed appropriate for, and relevant to the twentieth century, the doctrinal and scriptural authority of the Anglican Church will remain at their present low ebb.

4

Moral Authority

I

The notion of the church's moral authority over the beliefs and conscience of the individual has been touched upon at various points in the previous chapters, but although clearly related to the other forms of authority we have examined, it is a sufficiently distinct entity to warrant a separate discussion. At this stage it should perhaps be pointed out that the term 'moral authority' is intended to cover not merely the church's authority in moral and ethical matters, but rather that sense of authority which is derived from a perception of an individual or organization as having a superior competence to my own in certain matters, as a result of which I am willing voluntarily to accord them a measure of authority over me. Certainly moral and ethical issues would come into this sphere, but equally obviously 'moral authority' can be accorded on any issue whatever.

That said, the other dimension of authority with which this moral authority is most closely bound up is that of creeds and doctrines, and the church's assertion of moral authority (and the willingness of Christians to grant it) has been in large measure derived from this primary assumption of its right to prescribe the nature of correct belief and the penalties (whether spiritual or temporal) of failing to conform to such a belief. Clearly, if I can once be persuaded

66

of the church's right to prescribe my beliefs, and if these beliefs carry with them certain standards and expectations together with penalties for default (whether exercised here or hereafter) then I am quite likely also to accord that church a certain authority over other aspects of my life – if only for safety's sake!

Historically, the church's attitude has been very much that of assuming itself to be the final arbiter in such matters as the life-style of its members, and the 1662 *Book of Common Prayer* appears to have been conceived as a more-or-less complete handbook to correct belief and moral orientation in virtually every conceivable circumstance, as a glance at almost any of the less frequently used occasional offices will confirm. 'The Order for the Visitation of the Sick' exemplifies this doctrinal and moral vigour excellently, and the way in which they are yoked together (and the uncompromising authoritarianism of their expression) helps to explain why it is not used more often today!

The sick person is given moral counsel concerning their sickness, its origins and its purpose:

Dearly beloved, know this, that Almighty God is the Lord of life and death, and of all things to them pertaining, as youth, strength, health, age, weakness, and sickness. Wherefore, whatsoever your sickness is, know you certainly, that it is God's visitation. And for what cause soever this sickness is sent unto you; whether it be to try your patience, for the example of others, and that your faith may be found in the day of the Lord laudable, glorious, and honourable, to the increase of glory and endless felicity; or else it be sent unto you to correct and amend in you whatsoever doth offend the eyes of your heavenly Father; know you certainly, that if you truly repent you of your sins, and bear your sickness patiently, trusting in God's mercy for his dear Son Jesus Christ's sake, and render unto him humble thanks for his fatherly visitation, submitting yourself wholly unto his will, it shall turn to your profit, and help you forward in the right way that leadeth unto everlasting life.[1]

Having thus been shown the right attitude to have concerning their illness, the sick person is then reminded that their sickness, and their response to it, is a part of their Christian witness, which depends also upon their right belief as well as upon their moral orientation:

Now therefore, taking your sickness, which is thus profitable for you, patiently, I exhort you, in the name of God, to remember the profession which you made unto God in your Baptism. And forasmuch as after this life there is an account to be given unto the righteous Judge, by whom all must be judged without respect of persons, I require you to examine yourself and your estate, both toward God and man; so that, accusing and condemning yourself for your own faults, you may find mercy at our heavenly Father's hand for Christ's sake, and not be accused and condemned in that fearful judgement. Therefore I shall rehearse to you the Articles of our faith, that you may know whether you do believe as a Christian man should, or no.[2]

There is little compromise made with the person's sickness, and little overt compassion. What is important (and what is therefore seen as the prime purpose of the Visitation) is the maintenance of the person's right belief and right attitude towards God even (and perhaps especially) in the midst of the temptation to rebellion which sickness may bring. Everything including their present sickness is ordered under the hand of God, and is therefore also subject to the ministrations and authority of the church.

A service such as this one for the sick offers a valuable insight into the faith and understanding of a previous age. Presumably there was nothing strange or repugnant about it to the seventeenth-century mind, and generations of people meekly submitted themselves to the church's heavy-handed pastoral and moral care without appearing to find their subjection to the church either unwarranted or demeaning. For us today, looking back at such things, it all appears archaic in the extreme, to say nothing of its also involving a complete denial of any individual autonomy. Seventeenth-century invalids may have welcomed the ministry of the church in such a form, but it is hard to imagine many of us today allowing ourselves to be lectured (or perhaps hectored would be more accurate) on our sickbeds in such a way!

It is clear, then, that in the moral sphere, as in so many others, something has changed in the intervening centuries, and that with it has changed also our perception of how far the church should be allowed to dictate our moral attitudes and responses to the ethical and quasi-ethical issues of life. How has this change come about, and what have been, and will continue to be its implications for the life of the church?

Dorothee Soelle offers a compelling interpretation of exactly how and why our attitudes to the church and its authority have changed, and although she relates her analysis specifically to the religious life of the individual it would apply equally well to the collective religious life of the church during the past century and a half. She identifies three distinctive phases in the religious life, beginning with the concept of the religious village, a kind of spiritual age of innocence in which '...the church stood at the center of social and intellectual life. Myths and legends, values and ethical norms, were rooted and centered in traditions which were simply accepted.'[3] From here many people emigrate to the 'city', which Soelle uses as an image of religionlessness in which '...most throw off their religious heritage and live as post-Christian citizens in a secular city'.[4] It is, however, the third and final phase which is the most interesting. Soelle comments: 'After the religious security in the village, after the religion-free departure into the cold city, people decide consciously for new forms of religion,'[5] and she draws attention to the two characteristic features of this phase:

> First, it is a conscious religious decision. The religion of the village was inherited; one was born into it. But the new forms of religion – whether they be Christian or Eastern or from some other cultural horizon – are consciously chosen. That religion today can no longer be inherited is a result of the Enlightenment and of this human migration into the city,[6]

and secondly:

> ...the decision in favour of a religious conviction happens critically, not naively. We do not accept everything; we act selectively, making choices....With the departure from the religious village, authority – of the pastor, scripture, or the official church – is gone; it cannot be reinstituted. Anyone who comes to a critical affirmation of faith after an intensive debate in the second phase is now also struggling for the development of new forms of religious life.[7]

One may disagree with Soelle that authority cannot be reinstituted – indeed it is the thesis of this study that a radically new form of authority can and must be found by the church if it is to retain its integrity – but this analysis, drawn not only from her observation but from her own spiritual experience, seems to me to be a particularly penetrating one. Soelle is careful not to overstate her case by suggesting that it reflects every aspect of our twentieth-century religious experience, but she does accurately pinpoint a fundamental shift in our underlying attitude towards religion, and with it towards the whole concept of religious and moral authority.

Her critique is also thoroughly in line with the general philosophical and sociological consensus regarding the rise of individualism in the centuries since, perhaps, Descartes; and the validity of her model is borne out by even a cursory glance at the society in which we live. Advertising, the media, personal mobility, the move from the extended to the nuclear family, and so on, have all contributed to the growth of a society in which a huge premium is set on the 'rights' and the 'expectations' of the individual. We are expected to think for ourselves and to make up our own minds with regard to politics, education, our life-style, our spending, our employment, and it is small wonder, therefore, that we have come to demand the same individual freedom of choice in matters moral and religious.

As usual it is probable that there have been both gains and losses in the process. It would appear to be valuable that each individual is now encouraged to bear more direct responsibility for his or her own life and decisions, but the obverse of this has been a lessening of any sense of one's corporate responsibility or responsibility towards others. I am now so bound up with my own fulfilment and self-becoming that, ironically, I have no time or energy left for anyone else's! Likewise, in the context of the church, it is certain that we live today with a psychologically more health-giving approach to spirituality, which recognizes our intrinsic worth and capabilities rather than ascribing all that is positive to God and all that is negative to ourselves. At the same time, it is questionable whether religious and moral individualism has yet contributed much to the overall well-being of society or of the church. In fact, for the church itself, the major effect of the development of individualism is that amidst all the ever-increasing appeals to the judgment of the individual conscience, it has become very difficult – and often well-nigh impossible – for the church to declare itself on any moral issue with any degree of consensus, clarity or authority.

It would no doubt be possible to trace exhaustively the moral and spiritual pronouncements of the church during, say, the twentieth century, and to evaluate both the pronouncements themselves and the response of the faithful towards them, and this may well be a worthy task for some future sociologist of religion, but there is little merit in embarking on the tedium of such a *magnum opus* here. Rather, it is sufficient for our purposes to consider briefly three recent areas of controversy within the church (and between the church and the rest of society) which illustrate the conflicts and doubts which beset the church at the present time concerning its moral authority over peoples' lives.

II

The three issues to be considered here have been chosen because they each reflect a different aspect of the difficulties which confront the church in this sphere. The first of them, the ordination of women, concerns the church's authority (both moral and legal) over its own members, and especially over its clergy; the second, marriage and divorce, has implications for the church's voice within the nation; and the third, homosexuality, reveals the church's acute difficulty in arriving at a common mind – or even a consistent policy – on some of the more emotive and less obviously clear-cut issues of morality and discipline.

First, then, the ordination of women. In the midst of the current tensions, and in the light of the high passions of the past twenty years or so, this has become a topic which one is hesitant to approach at all. So much has been written and said, and so much bad feeling exposed on all sides, that one is reluctant to broach the subject for fear of becoming accidentally caught up in the mêlée, or being 'adopted' unwillingly and unwittingly as a proponent of one cause or the other. In the argument which follows here, it is important to recognize that the rights and wrongs of the ordination of women are not at issue – it is irrelevant for our purposes whether the step was in the end justified or not. Rather, what is significant for us is the very real problem which the actual *manner* in which the debate and the final decision were handled has created for the Anglican Church and the Church of England in particular.

The problem, in fact, is multi-faceted, although the various elements are distinctly related, and the damage which has been inflicted on the church's sense of its own authority is readily apparent by comparison with the comparable situation in certain other provinces of the Anglican Communion.

The seeds of the present situation were sown a good many years ago, during the many sessions of debate in General Synod and in the church press which followed the original 1970s ruling that there was no theological objection 'in principle' to the ordination of women, and which then led in turn to the introduction of the necessary legislation in synod. In these debates (and in countless other less formal arenas) the argument quickly arose: even if there is no theological objection (a 'fact' which was widely and hotly disputed anyway), there is still a grave question mark over the authority of the Church of England – or indeed any part of the Anglican Communion – to proceed with the ordination of women on a unilateral basis. This argument arose from the ancient self-perception of Anglicanism as being a part of the 'one, holy, catholic and apostolic church', and it was argued that a move such as the ordination of women represented a break with the traditional faith and order of that church; that such a development could only be sanctioned (if at all) by the authority of a General Ecumenical Council of the Church Catholic; and that in the absence of such a Council, any more local decision was unwarranted and unauthorized. Thus from the beginning, doubt was cast, by the opposers of the move, on the future validity of any decision to proceed with the ordination of women.

As time went on, and the strength of opposition to the move (as well as the strength of feeling in favour of it) became evident, the Church of England found itself in something of a cleft stick. It had opened Pandora's Box, and now it had to find some means of dealing with the assorted furies which had emerged from it. To go backwards was impossible – once off, the lid could not be replaced – but equally, how was it possible to go forward? Admittedly it was a particularly intractable problem, for neither side was willing to give an inch, and the issue came to dominate not only the relevant allotted times for debate in General Synod, but even the manifestos of candidates for election to synod – their views on other issues (or even their suitability as synod members) became submerged beneath the prior question of whether they were or were not in favour of the ordination of women.

Caught in this situation, what was the Church of England to do? Eventually, under further pressure from the opponents of the measure, some sort of compromise emerged. Traditionally Anglicanism has been caricatured for its willingness to compromise – 'find an Anglican a fence and he will sit on it!' Much of this criticism has been ill-founded, and the broad-mindedness and all-encompassing nature of Anglicanism has proved, through the centuries, to be one of its greatest strengths. On this particular occasion though, it looks, with hindsight, as though the criticism and caricature have for once been justified, for here Anglicanism has sat on the fence and the fence appears promptly to have collapsed underneath it!

Briefly, the nature of the compromise was enshrined in the so-called 'conscience clause', by virtue of which anyone who felt compelled to resign their orders on the grounds of their opposition to women priests could claim a compensation package from the Church of England. At first sight this seems a humane and compassionate response to an intractable problem, but in reality it is fraught with dangers and potentially destructive implications, the majority of which do not yet seem to have been fully realized.

The initial question-mark which hangs over the wisdom of this conscience clause is what it says (or rather, as yet, merely implies, since no one has actually admitted as much) about the vows taken by the clergy at their ordination and at their various licensings and Institutions to which we have referred earlier in chapter 2. These vows are principally vows of obedience to the authority of the church in its decisions, and specifically, in one's Institution, vows of obedience to a particular bishop and his successors. The key phrase used is that one will be obedient in all things commanded which are 'lawful and honest'. There would appear to be only two possible interpretations of this vow in the light of the conscience clause (given that it also provides for alternative episcopal oversight in the form of the so-called 'flying bishops'): namely, either that the vow in question is considered no longer binding, and is therefore virtually meaningless in the first place; or – and even more damagingly – that the ordination of women is potentially not 'lawful and honest' and that therefore the vow of canonical obedience simply does not apply, a possibility to which we shall return later. Canon lawyers and apologists for the measure may wriggle as hard as they can, but it is difficult to see any more satisfactory interpretation than these, neither of which appears to do much to uphold either the authority or the wisdom of the Church of England.

Alongside this difficulty, there is the related (but logically distinct) implication that the conscience clause – whether for resignation or for alternative episcopal oversight – actually sets the individual conscience above the decision making machinery of the Church as the final arbiter of what is acceptable in the broadly 'moral' sphere. Enshrined now in synodical legislation is the principle that the individual has the moral right explicitly to deny the authority of the church to inform his own conscience on this issue – and ultimately, if on this issue, why not, in principle, on any other?

Finally, and potentially most destructive of all, is the implicit admission by the Church of England that it may never have had the right to accede to the ordination of women in the first place. The conscience clause is, in effect, a tacit admission that the Church of England may have been mistaken. Again, this may sound a very laudable thing to admit, and appears to chime in well with ideas about the necessary humility of the church and the acknowledgment of its own fallibility. However, the wisdom of taking a step and then in the same breath suggesting that it may be a false step is at least questionable. It places in jeopardy the authority of the Church of England to take that step in the first place – and if there was any doubt about that, then presumably it should never have been taken – and in consequence it raises a question-mark over the authority of the church in every sphere and decision, for who is any longer to say which decisions are valid and which are not? Certainly not the General Synod of the Church of England which has, through the conscience clause, already questioned its own validity as an executive and legislative body.

Turning to some of the other provinces of the Anglican Communion, it is possible to see even more clearly the negative consequences of this particular way of handling the issue. In the Church of Ireland, for example, the measure for the ordination of women was passed before the Church of England had taken this step, but many of the pitfalls of the English situation have thankfully been avoided – and this in spite of the fact that there is just as wide a spectrum of opinion on the matter in Ireland as there is in England. Admittedly a part of this relatively painless (or at least, non-divisive) history may be due to the relative sizes of the two churches, since the Church of Ireland is so small as to have much more of a 'family' feeling about it, and knows itself to be too small to be able to risk division over this or any other issue. At the same time, however, the issue in Ireland has been handled, I would suggest, at once more capably and more confidently. No mention has been made of any sort of a conscience clause, and just as before the measure, the advocates of women's ordination were bound by the authority of the church (in the sense of not inviting women priests from other parts of the Communion to celebrate the eucharist illegally), so too, after the measure, the opponents of it are bound by that same authority to continue to work within a church which has done something of which they disapprove – and not merely to work within it, but to do so in fellowship with those with whom they disagree. Mutual respect and a lack of antagonism and personal attack have been the order of the day, and the direct legislative authority of the church – unweakened by self-doubt in this case – has been thoroughly backed up by the more general moral authority of the church which has been able (largely) to set down the expectations and guidelines within which the measure has been implemented. By contrast, the church of England's own self-doubt on a legislative level has continued to place in question its wider moral authority over its clergy, with the result that the issue is still causing (and will continue to cause, unless the situation is resolved) untold hurt and resentment both to the supporters and to the opponents of women's ordination.

III

The prime impact of the ordination of women, at least in terms of authority and obedience, has been on the clergy, since lay people are not bound by any vow, and are therefore free to depart from any church (with whatever sorrows) which enacts legislation which they feel unable to accept. In contradistinction to this is the more wide-ranging debate surrounding the church's attitude to both marriage and divorce (and specifically the re-marriage of divorced persons in church) which clearly impinges as closely upon lay members of the church as it does on their clergy.

The idea that the church should re-think its approach to the whole subject of marriage is not a new one; indeed our present understanding of marriage and with it the church's insistence (until recently) on the need for a wedding to be hallowed by a church service, is little more than five hundred or so years old, and derives from just such a re-think by the church in the mediaeval era – a re-think in which so-called 'common law' marriages, previously held to be valid by the church, were effectively outlawed by the church's increasingly stringent requirement for a marriage to be solemnized in church. Thus the church's willingness to respond to a changing society and to question its own attitudes and requirements is not, by itself, a sign of diminished authority or uncertainty about itself and its role. It is rather, in principle, an entirely responsible attitude on the part of a church which has no wish to lose its witness to, and place in the society which surrounds it. That said, however, there are certain features of the Anglican Church's approach to the issues of divorce and marriage which

78

indicate that the church is actually experiencing a good deal of trauma in its attempts to discover and articulate its own moral authority.

In the specific case of the remarriage of divorced persons in church, the principal uncertainty appears to be in the effort (or lack of it) to discern where real authority lies or should lie. Does it rest with the incumbent of a parish (who has always been given a large measure of freedom to make his own decisions in his parish), or is he in turn subject to his bishop? Technically and legally there is no doubt that final authority belongs to the incumbent: he is empowered by law to conduct such a marriage if he wishes to do so without reference to anyone else at all – and this remains true even in provinces such as the Church of Ireland where no formal synodical (or even episcopal) ruling has been made approving of such marriages. At the same time, however, the guidelines which have been produced, usually on a diocesan basis, make it plain that it is assumed that the bishop possesses a measure of moral authority over his clergy. There is thus at present a built-in conflict between the clergyman's legal autonomy and his 'obedience' to his bishop, and it is evident that in many cases the moral authority of the bishop has been disregarded and therefore made, for all practical purposes, irrelevant. An authority which is not statutory and which carries no sanctions is not, it seems, an authority to which many people are willing any longer to listen.

This same question of the re-marriage of divorced persons in church carries with it also some potentially disturbing implications for the future. It is to be welcomed that the Church of England (together with various other provinces of the Anglican Communion) has made provision for such marriages to take place, for it is plainly unjust and hurtful – not to say un-Christian – to deny the offices of the church to someone on the sole ground that they, or their future partner, are divorced, regardless of the history and circumstances of that divorce. However, there is a danger for the future that if the church later takes the step of making re-marriage in church a 'right' (in the same way as all parishioners have the 'right' to be married in church for a first time) then it will effectively have renounced all its moral authority in this area. It may appear to be a delightfully liberal and un-judgmental step to take, but once taken, the church then has no say whatsoever in the way in which people conduct their personal lives. The 'judgment' of each case will always be difficult, but I venture to suggest that both for its own sake and that of its moral influence over its people, and for the sake of those people themselves – for whom total self-determination and freedom in moral issues is not an unmixed blessing – the church needs to leave room in the future for its moral teaching to be heard and to have some sort of a cutting edge left to it.

On the wider issue of marriage in general, the church is confronted by a similarly tricky problem. Up until perhaps one hundred years or so ago, the expectations of the church with regard to marriage were broadly in line with those of the bulk of the population. Toady that situation has changed, with marriages becoming less stable, fewer people deciding to celebrate their wedding in church, and fewer people deciding to marry at all. The church is therefore faced with a society which contains a substantial percentage (but a still declining one) of 'traditionally' married couples, and an increasing number of single-parent families, and most significantly of all, an increasing number of couples who are choosing co-habitation as a preferable option to marriage, and who may be attached to each other with varying degrees of commitment and permanence. In such a situation the church is presented with the problem which was touched on in the Introduction to this study, of risking appearing on the one hand, either over liberal and trendy, or on the other hand, out of touch or repressive. The difficulty of the position is compounded by the fact of the church wanting: (a) to adhere to (and be seen as adhering to) some sort of coherent moral position, and in particular to uphold the sanctity and the value of Christian marriage; and (b) to do so without alienating or implicitly devaluing the lives of all those who do not adhere to precisely this set of moral values.

To be fair to the church, it is not easy to see clearly where the right way forward may lie, and there are a number of issues involved which need careful consideration. Is 'Christian marriage' as traditionally understood the only morally acceptable form of union between a man and a woman? And even if it is not, is it still to be seen as 'superior' or 'preferable' to any other form of loving commitment between people? Is the issue indeed primarily a moral one, or is it more of a practical one in terms of establishing what pattern of living will make for the most stable and fulfilling life-style? Similarly, are there moral considerations (such as love, compassion and trust) which outweigh the traditional *moralistic* division between marriage and 'living in sin'? All of these are questions which the church is having to address as it seeks to find a voice on the subject of marriage, and the tremendous difficulty of doing so satisfactorily has been recently demonstrated by the appearance of the Church of England Working Party's report, *Something to Celebrate*.[8] Enough has been said both for and against this report elsewhere for it to require no extensive discussion here, but both the report itself and the responses which it has aroused are enough to indicate that the church's future path (and the status of its moral authority) in the sphere of marriage are currently a topic of much uncertainty and consequently much speculation. It is too early yet to predict how this vociferous debate will be resolved, but whatever happens it is plain that in the current climate it is (and will continue to be) difficult for the church to claim a coherent measure of moral authority even over the lives of its members (let alone over those who claim no allegiance to the church) in a society which is thoroughly pluralist, and when, in addition, the church is rightly concerned not to lose touch entirely with that society.

By way of conclusion concerning the questions of marriage and divorce, I would simply suggest one possibility. Perhaps a part of the reason why the Anglican Church is finding its position so taxing and so threatening at present is that it is addressing the various issues which impinge on its moral authority in a somewhat piecemeal fashion. That is, it is attempting to respond to a whole variety of issues (including all of those raised in this chapter) individually, and does not appear as yet to have asked itself the prior question of where its claim to any moral authority on any issue is derived from: where can any moral voice conceivably be located with *any* degree of integrity or authority today?

This is a question which will be addressed in chapter 7, and it is a question which the Anglican Church may well find it imperative to answer satisfactorily if it is to speak with any confidence or integrity on similar issues in the future.

IV

The church's ability to find an answer to the above question might also make possible a more coherent response to the third of the themes under discussion here, that of homosexuality. As with a number of the other emotive and divisive issues touched on in this study, I am not primarily interested here in establishing what the church should be saying about it. In other words, whether homosexuality is 'right' or 'wrong', or whether it is not itself a moral issue at all, is not under discussion here. Instead, what is at stake here is the question of how the church comes to make any moral pronouncement at all (whichever way it may decide) and how this can be done with a measure of real moral authority – without which the voice of the church becomes merely an opinion, an opinion which may be taken up or discarded just like any other opinion.

Leaving aside then, exactly what the church should say about the practice of homosexuality, it is evident that what the church has in fact said about it has revealed the church's own current confusion about the status of its own authority, both in a disciplinary sense, and more importantly in a moral sense.

This confusion has arisen because in its pronouncements on the subject of homosexuality the church appears to have different standards and expectations for lay people and for clergy. In its general attitude, then, the church's 'official' policy is that the practice of homosexuality is not condemned. It is broadly accepted, and the same standards of loyalty, faithfulness and love may be enjoined upon homosexual partners as upon heterosexual partners. There is a slight confusion even here, however, in that whilst it is not actually condemned, neither is homosexuality actively approved of, and one gets the impression that it is in some fashion or other merely tolerated, which seems in either case an inadequate response: if homosexuality is 'wrong' then toleration is going too far; and if homosexuality is fully acceptable, then mere toleration is unfair and inadequate as a response to it.

Putting this initial confusion to one side, the church's general attitude to homosexuality is one of toleration, and much language is used about 'affirming' and 'encouraging' the values of love and fidelity and so on in all human ties and affections. One may or may not agree with this, but it is at least reasonably consistent as far as it goes.

The problem arises with the church's attitude to practising homosexuality on the part of the clergy. By contrast with all the language of affirmation used about lay people, clerical homosexuality is definitely beyond the pale – although again it must be acknowledged that there are tacit exceptions to this attitude which simply serve to muddy the water a little further. This is made plain even before ordination, in the ruling (not always adhered to) that anyone who has openly acknowledged that they are in a practising homosexual relationship will not be ordained, and it is equally re-affirmed thereafter by the very real threat of disciplinary action against any clergyman who is discovered to be in such a relationship. Quite apart from the fact that this merely drives clerical homosexuality underground, it is not only inconsistent but nonsensical that the church should lay down different standards for clergy and lay people. It is also thoroughly destructive of the church's integrity in the realm of moral authority.

For what is the church actually supposed to be saying in this two-headed pronouncement on homosexuality? Is it really advocating the position that homosexuality is acceptable among lay people but not among the clergy? That this is really the mind of the church seems very hard to believe, and one can only hope that such a curious and ludicrous double standard does not represent the settled view of the church. It may be less flattering in the short term but it is more hopeful in the long term to suggest that this anomaly arises from some very muddle-headed logic which may one day be sorted out coherently.

But even if the church is not really saying this, then what is its strange present attitude actually proclaiming? To which half of its personality should one attach the most weight? Should one assume that the church is expressing its true opinion in its attitude towards the clergy, or in its approach to lay people? In either case, a major dilemma arises. If the underlying attitude is that homosexuality is 'wrong' (as appears to be the case if one attaches weight to the situation with the clergy), they why is it permitted, and indeed cautiously affirmed, for lay people? Conversely, if homosexuality is perceived as 'right' or 'acceptable' (as is evinced by this affirmation of lay homosexuality) then why is the church attempting to impose sanctions on its clergy for doing something which, while it may depart from people's traditional expectations, is actually not in itself immoral or wrong?

It certainly looks as though in the future (and hopefully in the near future) the church will have to address the issue of homosexuality afresh, and attempt to come to a consistent mind on the matter. As yet there is no indication as to what this reassessment may produce (although there is plenty of pressure in both directions), and the current situation simply serves to highlight the confusion which so regrettably hinders the church either from reaching a definite mind on so many moral issues, or from articulating them with any degree of confidence or certainty in the public arena.

V

The three issues which we have chosen to highlight here have each illustrated specific areas in which the Anglican Church is experiencing a crisis both of conscience and confidence in the broadly 'moral' realm. As a final illustration, however, I propose to take an issue which is at once more personal and far more wide-ranging in its implications for the moral authority of the church. It is drawn from my own parochial experience, and, importantly, it relates to no one specific issue of behaviour or practice, but rather to the general perception of the church as having

– or not having – any moral authority over the lives of its members.

The occasion was that of a recent confirmation, when after consultation with my bishop, I refused to present two candidates. The grounds for doing so were substantial: neither candidate had been in church for over a year (not even a token appearance during the period of the confirmation classes), and they appeared to have no interest whatsoever either in forming or developing at least some sort of a relationship with God, or even in attending church occasionally once confirmed. I therefore explained to their parents that the two candidates did not seem to be ready for confirmation, since it did not appear to mean anything to them, and that I felt that they would benefit from waiting for at least a year. Confirming them now would be somewhat meaningless as they appeared to have no desire to profess the Christian faith for themselves, nor to take their place as adult members of the church.

The response to this was two-fold: on the part of the parents (and a very few other members of the congregation) I was told that such a step was unheard of, and that I had no right to 'judge' their children in such a way; by contrast, the response of the bulk of the parish was supportive of the decision, but again equally surprised that such a thing was possible, it never having been heard of before in the parish.

What this small incident reveals is simply that on the part of many people in the church there is no longer a living sense of the church as having any moral authority over their lives – so that they are extremely surprised, even if also pleased, to find that such an authority can still be invoked; but also that as far as some people are concerned, there is a strong feeling that the church should not have such an authority at all – that the church is there merely to do their bidding and to be there when they want it, and not to rock their comfortable boat by having the temerity to suggest anything about how they live their lives or conduct their personal or business affairs.

In the day-to-day microcosm of parish life, as well as in the larger concerns of the wider church, it is plain that through its own internal confusions and divisions as well as through people's negligible expectations of its moral influence, the church is currently having to come to terms with a substantial decline in its perceived moral authority both over the lives of its own members and in the increasingly pluralist and individualist milieu of contemporary society.

5

Anglicanism in Crisis

I

During the course of the previous chapters we have examined in some detail a number of the ways in which Anglicanism has seen its traditional authority being eroded and undercut in the past few generations, and it is appropriate at this point to consider something of the overall effect of this erosion. Just as with the particular instances which we have looked at, the general effect upon Anglicanism of its loss of authority appears to have been to leave Anglicanism in a state of uncertainty, not merely about the specific issues we have touched on, but more seriously, about itself and its own identity and validity. As a Communion – and especially in certain provinces – Anglicanism is in danger of becoming directionless, colourless and motivated rather by reactive than by proactive stimuli – by fear rather than by conviction.

A telling example of this 'Anglican drift' would be the so-called 'Decade of Evangelism'. The inspiration for this came from the 1988 Lambeth Conference, and the bishops enthusiastically issued the call for the 1990s to be such a decade, although some have since regretted it and voiced the opinion that the idea was ill-conceived. In all probability the reason for this change of heart on their part was the salutary discovery that Anglicanism was not ready for – or not capable of implementing – such a programme at the present time; and that this is so would seem to be borne out by the rather shaky progress of the decade, certainly within the churches of the British Isles. I do not doubt that there are individual churches and groups of churches which have responded, but the overall picture of the four 'home' Anglican churches does not immediately seem to be one of a church which is totally committed to evangelism or which is notably more vibrant than it was at the start of the decade. Indeed, in many instances, the momentum seems to have flagged considerably, and the decade is in danger of running out of steam when it is barely more than half completed. For the most part there does not appear to be any great confidence in the air, and no real sense of what it might mean to be a church with a mission and a vision, or even of what such a vision might be composed. In the middle of a decade which was conceived as a dynamic and forward moving challenge, there is a disheartening lack of direction. The waters of Anglicanism appear, temporarily at least, to have stagnated. Of this stagnation, Stephen Sykes comments tellingly, and with particular reference to the English situation:

> Has not the Church of England become a Church without a structure of authority capable of speaking with authority, and worse, a Church without vision, a Church which has ceased to believe that its corporate decisions could be guided by the Holy Spirit.[1]

Admittedly Sykes is here reflecting 'popular' opinion of the church, rather than giving his own personal assessment, but his comments are none the less damning for that.

The result of all this lost confidence, authority and self-belief is that the church has, almost without knowing it – and certainly without acknowledging it – moved into a new phase. This phase is one in which the emphasis is on survival rather than on growth, mission, or service. It is intrinsically an inward-looking rather than an outward-looking phase, in which the church's attention is consumed with the problem of simply keeping itself in being – and yet of course this is harder than ever when there is already such a loss of confidence and identity as we have outlined. In such circumstances it becomes hard even to know what it is that we are trying to keep alive.

Thus, in a way which we have never witnessed before, we find ourselves today in a church which has changed its whole nature and its approach to the world around it, in that now for the first time it finds that it has almost to supplicate for the attention of that world, and does not have the confidence any longer to command that attention by the vibrancy of its life or preaching.

The church's response to the lack of attention paid to it is to attempt to devise ever new ways to 'appeal to' or 'attract' particular groups of people towards the church – the young; the newly married; parents and toddlers and so on. It does so by offering a special service, an event, a party, a disco, or any one of many hundreds of different ideas. Intrinsically there is nothing wrong with any of these events, but one cannot help feeling that there is something missing or seriously awry at the heart of things if the church has permanently to resort to an endless stream of treats – or even worse of gimmicks – in order to 'attract' people to the gospel of Jesus Christ and to the fellowship of the 'one, holy, catholic and apostolic church'. Special services and events are all very well, but I would question whether they should have to constitute (as they so often do) the church's main means of outreach, so that it appears as though the church is having to institute a recruiting drive for new members and must be made as attractive and racy as possible for them. The church is, or should be, a somewhat different kind of organization from the local badminton or bridge club.

Such a life-style appears to be an 'inauthentic' one for the church, by which I mean one that is not true to its own fundamental identity and task, and for all its occasional gains in terms of new 'recruits' to its various activities on offer, it is one of the features of the church which helps to explain its present lack of esteem in our society. The church has resorted to the tactics of the entrepreneur and the media, and these are not, in the end, appropriate for it as a means of outreach, for the message which such tactics covertly imply is actually the wrong one. All the various drives towards new membership may be wrapped up in the trappings of the gospel, but what is being 'advertised' is not, first and foremost, the Good News of Jesus Christ, but the need of the church for new members. In the church's 'authentic' witness to the world there has always been – and must be again – a sense of confidence and a passionate belief in the value of the gospel to which it is witnessing, such that the church's witness is always *outward*: a witness for the sake of others. In other words, there must be the knowledge that the church is privileged to share in something so wonderful, that it must in turn want to share it with others. By contrast to this, the church's witness at present feels for the most part to be – if such a thing is logically possible – an inward-looking thing: that is, the church seems to be 'witnessing', or rather attempting to attract people, primarily because it is so unsure of itself and so afraid of declining numbers that it needs to draw new people in for the sake of its own survival, rather than to share with them its Good News.

Clearly, the above remarks do not apply to the whole of the Anglican Church, and there will be at any time, some places and some congregations whose life and witness are, thankfully, in the authentic mould. However, there does appear, for the most part, to be something of a malaise within Anglicanism today, and the 'inauthenticity' which I have described is certainly both a part and a symptom of it. It is not the first time that such a thing has happened in the life of the church, and hopefully the Anglican Church will again emerge from it. If this is to happen, and if we are to come out of it, then the church needs to find again its confidence in itself, derived from its confidence in the Good News of Jesus Christ, and from the experience of the value of living and preaching that Good News. Without this confidence of faith there is little hope of change, and without it little hope for the future in a largely hostile or indifferent world.

II

Before we can turn to the possibility of change and consider whence it might stem and how it might occur, however, it is essential to appreciate why it is that such change and new confidence is likely to prove extremely difficult to develop in the current state of Anglicanism. This is not to say that it will prove impossible, but merely that it is a problem to which there is no 'easy option' kind of an answer: it is a problem whose ramifications Anglicanism needs to consider carefully and courageously if the church is to emerge from it renewed and strengthened.

Given, then, that Anglicanism has lost so much of its authority, identity and confidence as a result of the various factors we have considered in previous chapters, why is it that the crisis has bitten so deeply, such that Anglicanism is finding it at present almost impossibly difficult to articulate a coherent response to almost any issue, or to shape and express a life-giving vision for the future?

In the Introduction to this study, reference was made to the important distinction which is to be drawn between the related concepts of the authority *of* the church, and authority *in* the church, and it is likely that much of the Anglican Church's difficulty in regaining its confidence and identity stems from a failure properly to appreciate the significance of this distinction. In essence, what has happened is that the two concepts have been presumed to be related in precisely the opposite fashion to that in which they are in fact related. Thus the concept of authority *in* the church has been presumed to be logically prior to that of the authority *of* the church: or, to put it another way, the church's internal ordering has been presumed to be logically prior to the confidence and conviction with which it must proclaim its gospel – a gospel which itself, of course, claims authority over those who hear it. This way of ordering things sounds logical enough – that the church should set its own house in order *before* it attempts to amend or improve its relationship and witness to the world. In fact, however, the two concepts of authority should be related the other way around: the church's authority and self-identity are prior to its internal authority, an inversion which has not yet been recognized by the church.

This is a subject to which Stephen Sykes devotes substantial attention in the context of an extended discussion of the refusal of Anglicanism to enunciate a coherent Anglican ecclesiology, and he comments acerbically:

The second reason for the failure to respond to the charge of incoherence is the absorption of so much time and effort, both leading up to and following the 1988 Lambeth Conference, in a largely fruitless effort to clarify the subject of authority in Anglicanism. It ought to have been obvious that it was impossible to arrive at theological or practical conclusions on authority *in* the Church without the help of a theology *of* the Church. But it has proved otherwise. And we have been painfully

93

learning in the last decades, not least through ecumenical relationships, that we cannot borrow a doctrine of the Church from any other Communion of Christendom, and pass it off as Anglican with a few minor adjustments. The very refusal of Anglicanism to oblige its critics by withering or splintering to death may in due course drag us, however reluctantly, to the task of ecclesiological self-interpretation.[2]

This study is written in the belief that Stephen Sykes is correct in his assertion, and his ideas would chime in very closely with the argument here that the church has inverted the primacy of the two concepts of authority, for clearly what Sykes refers to as the need for an Anglican ecclesiology is intimately related to my own search here for a new foundation for the authority of the church. In the past, living in a hierarchically ordered world and society, the church had no need of such a search – the authority which was accorded to it by that society and which it assiduously gathered to itself was quite sufficient to provide it with a recognizable identity and with a good deal of self-confidence – sometimes, perhaps, too much. Today, however, that identity and confidence have crumbled, and Sykes rightly divines the need for a new self-reappraisal and re-articulation of Anglican identity. This present work is not intended to be the definitive answer to Sykes' challenge: it is not a fully worked out ecclesiology. It does, however, deal with many of the same questions, and the issues covered here would form the groundwork for any more extended and properly doctrinal study of the identity of Anglicanism. A study such as the present one is, in a very real sense, a prerequisite of any response to Sykes' call for an Anglican ecclesiology, in that what will be identified here is the foundation for such a work – a grasp of exactly *where* a distinctively Anglican self-understanding might be rooted.

One consequence of this will be a renewed authority for (because of a renewed identity of) the Anglican Church, and, revitalized by this, Anglicanism may then be able, at last, to come to terms with the secondary issue of authority *in* the church which has similarly bedevilled it for so long.

III

What, then, should be the response of Anglicanism to Sykes' critique, and to the disintegration of identity and confidence which we have traced here? In detail there may well turn out to be all sorts of possible courses, but in more general terms there would appear to be two major poles of response; that is, any effort to rebuild Anglican identity and confidence is likely to be predominantly either backward-looking or forward-looking. Each of these possibilities requires some elucidation here.

First, those efforts which are essentially backward-looking are all – and will continue to be – in different ways attempts to regain the kind of status and authority which the church once enjoyed. This is the pattern of approach which would tend to be espoused by the more conservative elements within the church, and one hears a good deal of their various voices even in the present day, although this is a voice which may well also strengthen in the future. Thus there is a number of church societies and less formal groupings whose primary reason for existence is to preserve something in the life of the church, or in some cases even to resurrect something. Not surprisingly the majority of these societies and groupings are to be found at the more extreme evangelical and Anglo-Catholic ends of the church spectrum, since each of these wings would tend to have an innate conservatism about it, based either on the unchanging witness of scripture or of church tradition, doctrine and order. Their characteristic stance would be to issue a call for a 'firm attitude' or a scriptural/moral/ doctrinal response to a particular issue, and to be concerned to uphold 'traditional church teaching' on such an issue, be it liturgical, theological or ethical.

One could choose almost any of these groups, but a good representative example would be ABWON (Action for Biblical Witness to our Nation) founded and since guided by the Revd Tony Higton. ABWON itself is a relatively recent newcomer on the scene as societies go, but it was founded as a direct response to a perceived need for just such a firm and traditional line on a number of issues, among them marriage, divorce and homosexuality, the church's official confusion on which we have discussed previously. ABWON itself would in all probability deny the epithet of backward-looking, but since its call is for the church to say the same things and on the same grounds as it has said them in the past, this description would not seem to be entirely unfair.

The same concern is also reflected in the debate which surfaces every time a bishop (and especially a diocesan bishop) retires: who will be appointed and what is his stance ecclesiastically? Sometimes what seems to be most important is whether so-and-so is 'conservative evangelical' or 'Anglo-Catholic', a traditionalist or a liberal, rather than whether he is actually a suitable person with the appropriate gifts to be appointed as a diocesan bishop. Depending on your standpoint, an inept evangelical can look preferable to a capable liberal, for example!

In each case, the central aim is uppermost – to maintain the *status quo*, and add a bit of stiffening to the church in the hope that it will regain something of its lost authority and identity by so doing – and the desire which motivates this aim is entirely understandable. Seeing, quite correctly, a church which has lost its way, these conservative individuals and groups naturally wish to take a stand wherever it is that they feel the church has failed. They see too a world which largely ignores the church and finds its inertia laughable, and they therefore react by attempting to reconstruct the more authoritarian and sterner church of a previous age, at which no one had dared to laugh, in the hope that such a church may turn out to be effective again. Their passionate concern for the church is laudable, but I for one would question whether their response of backward-looking conservatism is actually the most appropriate or the most effective one. For it is an effort to return to what is perceived to have been a golden age, a kind of ecclesiastical Garden of Eden, and there is nothing more certain than that paradise, once lost, can never be regained. What is most likely to happen to these groups (for all their good intentions) is that they will indeed succeed in remaining unchanged but will simply fossilize in the process, becoming completely out of touch with a society whose every change they disparage, and consequently finding themselves to be completely irrelevant to all of the equally changed needs and issues of that society. They may pride themselves on occupying the moral high ground, but that ceases to be of much practical value and becomes a very lonely eminence if no one else is any longer interested in climbing their particular mountain.

The diametrically opposite response to this backward-looking one is equally possible and equally understandable. This is to acknowledge – and indeed to take almost as a truism – the inappropriateness of past methods and solutions to the problems of today, and to look resolutely forward towards what is new for any source of new life or hope for the church. And again this has proved to be a popular option. At present, there is equally a number of groups and individuals for whom there is nothing to look backwards to and everything to look forwards to. The essence of this endeavour is to forge a new identity for the church which is relevant and workable in twentieth-century society and which does not depend for its validity on the vanished resources of past ages which cannot now be recaptured.

Among those involved in this radically forward-looking quest are the doctrinally minimalist theologians discussed in chapter 3, and broadly aligned with them would be organizations such as the Sea of Faith Network, whose concerns are not only theological but also practical, such as finding a meaningful approach to prayer which allows Christians to join hands with those of other faiths also. For them, the way forward is one of finding an identity almost beyond the church – letting go of all that used to be distinctive and allowing a shared humanity and a shared concern for the life of the spirit to be the focus of a new and all-inclusive religious fellowship.

Again, given the present divisions, squabbles and differences of Christendom, there is a certain appeal in this idea. Anything which creates a bond and an identity between people rather than dividing or confusing them is almost bound to look attractive. However, it may equally be questioned whether such an unequivocally one-directional approach is the most constructive. The ultimate wisdom of thoroughgoing radicalism in theology has already been queried in this study, and there are obvious dangers involved for the church in any attempt to sever all ties with the past. At best there is the probability that together with what may be the dross, something – or indeed much – of value may be wantonly discarded; and at worst there is the possibility that like a shop I once saw, there may be a 'Business as usual during alterations' sign up, but the alterations have been so drastic that the shop has actually collapsed.

These dangers notwithstanding, I would suggest that the balance of credibility lies more with those who would look forward than with those who would look backwards, for the church, no more than any other organization, can never recapture a past age or live with a permanent and debilitating sense of nostalgia. Perhaps what modern radical trends indicate is that there will be many false starts in the effort to identify and give shape to the distinctive voice of Anglicanism today, but this, of course, does not itself invalidate the attempt. It merely confirms the intractability of the problem and the difficulty involved in finding an adequate and compelling response to it. We shall argue in chapter 7, however, that there remains a further possibility, which whilst leaning towards the future does not invalidate or ignore the previous history of Anglicanism or deny such of its insights as may still be salutary for the church of today.

In the meantime, and before this alternative can be developed further, there is one final issue which must be addressed. This is the relationship between the concepts of 'power' and 'authority', for whether one's response to the crisis surrounding Anglicanism is intrinsically forward or backward looking will in all probability depend upon one's understanding of these two concepts and one's instinctive preference for one or the other of them. What the shape of Anglicanism will be in the future will in large measure depend upon whether or not it can renounce any quest for power such as it once had, and whether or not it can find the courage to venture forth into a new era of powerlessness and seek to find a new authority there. To these related, but crucially distinct concepts, we must therefore turn.

6

Authority or Power?

I

Just as there is a distinction to be made between the authority *of* the church and authority *in* the church, so too there is an important difference between the related ideas of authority and power. The fact that the two terms are closely related means that there is a danger of their being used synonymously, and this both impoverishes our language and leads to confusion as to what is actually meant. It is essential, then, to distinguish carefully what is intended by the two words, and to see more precisely what are the similarities and differences both between the words themselves and between the nuances and overtones which each bears.

Part of the lack of clarity which is often found in the way these terms are used stems from their basic dictionary definitions. The Oxford English Dictionary, for example, does not make particularly clear the different shades of meaning which each has, and unhelpfully uses 'power' as one of the principal terms in its definition of 'authority': 'Power to enforce obedience' is its first definition. This may be true to the roots of the two words, and even to a very limited range of their meaning – 'authority' *can* mean this sometimes – but it does not accurately reflect the way in which they would most often be used. Thus regardless of their precise application in this study, it is evident that we do frequently distinguish sharply between them even in an ordinary everyday context. You may have the *authority* to tell me to behave in a particular way or to do your bidding, and yet it is quite conceivable that I may have the *power* to refuse. Here, authority and power are quite clearly not the same thing at all, and the two terms in the above sentence cannot be reversed without creating semantic nonsense.

In this kind of usage, which would not be at all unusual, and in no way strains our normal understanding of the words, each of them self-evidently carries an entirely different set of resonances. A useful distinction, which would more accurately reflect this normal usage, would be to suggest that the concept of authority involves having the 'right' (whether moral or statutory) to do or say something or to request others to comply with a directive, and may also have a bearing on the *gravitas* of the pronouncement or action, and that the essence of power is that of having the *de facto* ability to make something happen regardless of the rights and wrongs which may be involved. A distinction such as this one is therefore to be understood as underlying the discussion here: a relationship between the two terms is not denied, but the characteristic nuances of each are seen to be substantially different.

Historically there is no doubt that throughout much of its existence the church has wielded a considerable amount of power in the sense in which it has been defined here. It has had the ability both to make decisions which affect the life of the society around it, and to enforce the obedience of the faithful. Today, however, this is no longer the case: the church has lost its power, and since its authority was largely founded on that power, it has discovered that its authority has vanished also. To refer back to the discussion in the previous chapter, this loss of power is one of the main reasons why conservative backward-looking groups within the church tend to appear as something of an anachronism.

A 'hard line' church which must be heeded and obeyed is no longer possible in the way that it once was, and whatever stance these groups may call for, the church no longer has the outright power to back this call and to make anything happen or to force people to conform to its doctrinal or moral requirements. Thus the bare demand for such-and-such a stance comes to seem at once out of place in a changed climate, and curiously empty of any realistically workable content. It should be noted, however, that this does not imply that the church cannot any longer 'stand' for or witness to any moral or spiritual excellence. It most certainly can, as we shall argue in chapter 7: it is merely that the church can no longer do so in this outmoded fashion of simply demanding a return to this or that standard of behaviour or doctrine.

Not surprisingly, therefore, conservative elements within the church will tend to bemoan the fact of the church's loss of power, for it deprives their own particular cause of virtually all of its practical credibility: the things they stand for may in some instances be admirable, but things simply cannot happen any longer in the way that they would like. Their voice is ultimately doomed to be a sterile one in the modern world. In spite of this, though, it is certain that this loss of power is essentially a good thing, both on a theological and spiritual level and on a practical level.

Theologically and spiritually the removal of power creates a space for the exercise of freedom and goodness, and for the spiritual and moral growth of humanity – a fact which is often not appreciated by those who regret the passing of the 'good old days' of morality and 'Christian standards' in society. Regardless of whether they are actually right that modern society is more 'immoral' than the society of previous ages – a 'fact' which is highly questionable – it can convincingly be argued that in this past era of so-called 'morality', people were not in fact being good or moral, they were simply behaving in a certain way to avoid the penalties of doing otherwise. They were not making a free and conscious moral choice in favour of what they perceived as goodness, but instead they were largely coerced into this behaviour by the pressure of the society and church within which they lived, and which had stringent sanctions available for the chastisement of transgressors. It is only once the power of coercion is removed that people are then, for the first time, free consciously to choose their moral standards and to behave in a way which can rightly be described as 'good' or 'moral' at all.

Similarly, there is a real sense in which this loss of coercive power has allowed (or is allowing) humanity to grow up – not simply into morality but into responsibility. Previously people were effectively like over-protected children, shielded from all possible harm by being given no freedom to explore the world for themselves. They may have been safe, but they were also stunted. Now that the protective arm of power has been necessarily withdrawn, we are free to act according to our own lights, and to discover for the first time what personal responsibility means. As a consequence of our errors we may get hurt (just like a child who misjudges a step and falls over), but we shall at least be able to grow and develop – morally speaking learn to walk – in a way that was denied to us before.

There is, furthermore, an important reflection of these perceptions in our understanding of Christian doctrine, and in particular the doctrine of free will. Our relationship with God and our perception of his purpose in creation is rooted in the conviction that God created us as free and responsible beings in a morally non-deterministic universe, so that we might respond to him and be drawn towards him in love, rather than coerced by him into any kind of rigid pattern of pre-programmed behaviour. Indeed, just how central such an understanding is becomes clear as soon as any attempt is made to construct any kind of a theodicy. One of the main arguments in almost any theodicy is that the presence of evil and suffering in the world is a necessary concomitant of a free universe and a free humanity, for there is no possibility of 'goodness' in a universe which is not free, since no moral term (whether goodness, love or anything else) has any meaning without its opposite – exactly as was suggested in microcosm by our previous discussion of the so-called 'morality' of a previous age. Presumably God could have created a universe in which no one could ever come to any harm, and in which no one was free to do anything except what he wished them to do, but such a universe would have no moral status or value whatsoever – indeed, the whole concept of morality would be entirely meaningless in such a universe. Moral value can only be ascribed to any action or utterance when it is freely chosen – and when there is an alternative which has equally been freely rejected – and the system cannot be short-circuited by the exercise of coercion. A response to God of freely-offered love cannot, by definition, be coerced.

Theologically, then, the church's loss of coercive power is to be welcomed, for the exercise of coercion by the church represents a denial of God's purpose in creation. No doubt the sixteenth-century inquisitors believed firmly that they were doing God's work, but today we rightly see in them only a grotesque and revolting caricature of the church's mission of drawing souls to God.

The demise of the church's power carries with it not only theological and spiritual, but also practical benefits. Just as, on the moral and theological plane it leaves room for goodness and moral values, so too on a practical level it leaves a space for the distinctive exercise of a genuine authority rather than power. Indeed, I would go so far as to argue that it is only in a situation of powerlessness that the notion of authority can be adequately realized, for in the sense in which the terms are used here it is extremely difficult to envisage a way in which they could realistically co-exist as separate discernable entities. Throughout the history of the human race, power, when it is real, has tended to swallow up the more subtle quality of authority: indeed, if *de facto* you discover that you have power, then you no longer need authority – with or without it you can still make things happen and make people obey you in the way you wish them to do. If the Anglican Church is to find and define a new authority, then, it must learn first not only to accept, but even to rejoice in its contemporary state of relative powerlessness, for whilst this is a material loss, it is equally a spiritual and moral gain.

II

Thus far in this discussion it may appear that we have disowned the concept of power altogether. This is not, in fact, the case, and to do so would be naive in the extreme, for a measure of power is a fact of life in any organization including the church. The sense in which we have disowned power here is that of the church's former directly coercive power exercised over the whole of society – a form of power which has been largely external in its effects. Similarly we have disowned the centralized and direct power of the hierarchy over the members of the church – that is, power as an entity which resides solely in the hands of a few and which is exercised by them without the possibility of correction or outside restraint. However, this is not to deny that there will inevitably be some power residing in the church, in its internal organization, even if not in its relations with the world around it. Human nature being what it is, it is hard to see how any organizational structure could function effectively without a modicum of power inherent within it. Any organization must be able to make decisions and implement them effectively. What is important, if this power is not to interfere with the integrity of authority, is that it should be a power which is accountable, and the abuse of which, if it occurs, can be readily curtailed. In what fashion then, can this more moderate exercise of power be related to the wider concept of the authority of the church?

In order to establish the relationship between them, we need in the process to indicate more clearly the parameters of the authority of the church. Far and away the most important of these is that this authority should always be understood as a diffuse and dispersed authority; one which does not reside merely in a few individuals who can then, of course, quickly convert this authority into outright power whenever they so wish.

That authority must be dispersed in this way was recognized by the bishops at the Lambeth Conference of 1948:

It [authority] is distributed among Scripture, Tradition, Creeds, the Ministry of the Word and Sacraments, the witness of saints, and the *consensus fidelium*, which is the continuing experience of the Holy Spirit through His faithful people in the Church. It is thus a dispersed rather than a centralized authority having many elements which combine, interact with, and check each other; these elements together contributing by a process of mutual support, mutual checking, and redressing of errors or exaggerations to the many-sided fullness of the authority which Christ has committed to his Church. Where this authority of Christ is to be found mediated not in one mode but in several we recognize in this multiplicity God's loving provision against the temptations to tyranny and the dangers of unchecked power.[1]

To this passage, Stephen Sykes adds the percipient comment that:

> Unless I am very much mistaken, this is the only kind of authority justifiable in the universal Church of Christ, and is one which we as Anglicans have every reason to explore, to expound and to defend, without a hint of that curiously smug self-deprecation which has so paralysed us in our public theological stances of late. Its essential feature is the recognition of the richness and historicity of the divine revelation. The distribution of God's gifts to the whole Church means that there are *voices* of authority, not one unambiguous, unequivocal voice of authority. It means that these voices of authority are the consequence of the call of God to every Christian believer to embody the saving Gospel in his or her own life, and to receive the empowering gift of the Holy Spirit to that end.[2] [Sykes' italics.]

Again, as we observed earlier, this is a very different understanding of authority from that of those who would look backwards in history and seek to regain the authority (and power) of a past age. For them, authority needs to be centralized if it is to work, and that is precisely what is being denied here. Again, Stephen Sykes issues a timely warning on this score:

> ...the Church of England is also a Church under pressure, and one can certainly hear opinions advanced in favour of radically simplified canons and structures of authority. We have, however, a long history of *not* simplifying these matters. We could do very much worse than ponder the highly differentiated account of authority given by Richard Hooker in the late sixteenth century. For him divine wisdom is imparted to humanity in diverse ways,

not in one, and the interpretation of the sacred scriptures requires the divine endowment of reason, in persons consulting, discussing and reasoning together in the community of the faithful.[3] [Sykes' italics.]

Such is very much the understanding of authority which is intended here, and whatever measure of direct power the hierarchy (or General Synod, or any other body) may or should have, it must only ever be exercised in the context of, and in the consciousness of, this wider authority of the whole Church under the hand of God through the guidance of his Holy Spirit.

III

Finally, and directly related to the presence of the Holy Spirit in the church, there is one sense in which a certain kind of 'power' is the complement – and also the creator – of the kind of authority espoused here.

Once again it is Stephen Sykes who offers a particularly useful analysis of exactly what this power is and where it is located. Two of the factors which he singles out in the course of this discussion are:

(i) We acknowledge, and rejoice in the reality of divine power, the power of the Holy Spirit, in the Church. This is the dynamic (*dynamis*) from which all exercise of authority proceeds, and in virtue of which every member of the body takes his or her part in the conflict with evil.

(ii) This power may also be spoken of as the power of the Gospel of Christ, and it is given not to a privileged few, a hierarchy or intellectual elite, but to the whole Church. Every Christian, therefore, exercises the authority bestowed on him or her by his or her reception and realization (in word and deed) of the Gospel.[4]

These two features are essential to the presence and exercise of this kind of power – that it is a power which is divine and not human, and that in the wisdom of God it is (as with the more general authority of the church which derives from it) a dispersed and not a centralized power.

The best word to convey the creative force involved in this kind of power is the biblical term which Sykes uses, *dynamis*, for this term recognizes that it is an entirely different conception of power from that which we have eschewed in our earlier discussion, and it is unfortunate that the English word 'power' has to do duty for both senses. The *dynamis* of which Sykes speaks represents an entirely different concept of power, one which is principally a motive power and not a coercive power. It is more akin (in so far as the comparison may be made at all) to the power of an internal combustion engine than to the power which I may be said to have over another person.

In the course of the various distinctions which have been drawn, and reflections on the nature of power and authority which have been made in this chapter, we may conclude that it is appropriate (and necessary for its well-being) that the church should eschew the exercise of any power which is, or threatens to become coercive, but that it is equally certain that the church *needs* to be filled with the dynamic power which Sykes identifies. It is, indeed I believe, this *dynamis* which, if it is truly present, will shine through the church's life and give credence to the authority of the church for which we have argued.

Thus far, then, we have established in some detail what is meant by the concept of authority as opposed to coercive power, and identified both the parameters for the exercise of a limited power within the church, and the need for a divine power informing, inspiring and motivating the whole. It now remains finally to establish in what the authority of the church might consist and where it might credibly be located, and to discern where the *dynamis* or motive power behind such an authority as we have envisaged may be said to lie.

7

A New Authority

I

At the end of the previous chapter we posed the question of where a new authority for the church might be located and in what it might consist. If the question is to be answered in such a way as to produce a coherent and credible understanding of authority for the contemporary church, then there are two dangers which must be avoided. The temptation will always be to retreat into what is known, to that which feels safe and secure, rather than to take the risk involved in treading new ground, and for the church the two familiar paths are scripture and tradition. Each of these is valuable, and indeed the concept of authority articulated here has a substantial measure of scriptural appeal, but neither scripture nor tradition must be allowed to become enslaving, and the dangers of scriptural fundamentalism and ultra-conservative traditionalism must both be avoided if the authority of the church is to prove flexible enough to survive in today's world.

If, then, an over-reliance on either of these two safe and familiar sources is to be denied to us, where can the church now realistically turn to locate its authority? A useful starting point is the historical Anglican understanding of dispersed authority outlined in the previous chapter, an excellent example of which is the Lambeth Conference statement of 1948 which was quoted there. This identifies six separate but related sources of authority: '...Scripture, Tradition, Creeds, the Ministry of the Word and Sacraments, the witness of saints, and the *consensus fidelium*, which is the continuing experience of the Holy Spirit through his faithful people in the Church'.[1]

A list such as this one would be typical of the Anglican approach to authority throughout the history of the Communion, and there is, as we have argued, a real value in this diffuse and un-centralized approach to authority. There is, however, one common factor behind all of these various sources of authority which binds them together and to which the church may therefore legitimately turn for a renewed validation of her authority. This factor is at once so obvious as to be in one sense already at the heart of the church's understanding of itself and its authority, but equally so obvious as never to have been fully taken into account and analysed in any search for authority. It is quite simply the person of Jesus Christ himself: attested to in scripture and creeds, and experienced as living and active in the lives of the saints and the faithful and in the ministry and worship of the church. Quite clearly the person of Jesus Christ has always been a presence within the church's understanding of its authority, but equally this has always been as he is mediated through the 'filter' of creeds, traditions and so on. What is needed today, however, is for the church to turn to a radically new understanding of Jesus Christ as the locus of its authority – one which is based not merely on Jesus as seen through creeds and dogmas, but one which is rather based upon the nature and ministry of Jesus as that is expressed both in scripture and equally importantly in Christian experience, and in which the church acquires authority only in so far as its life and ministry conform to the pattern and the mind of Christ.

In arguing for such a Christ-centred authority it should be stressed that we are not arguing merely for a renewed appeal

112

to scripture: it is not an appeal to any supposed final authority of scripture, although clearly the Jesus of the Gospels will inform and inspire the church's present experience. Such a rooting in scripture is important, as, for example, Stephen Sykes readily acknowledges:

...Anglicans are right to insist that we should under no circumstances lose contact with the biblical witness to the Church in its full historic reality. Processes in the Church cannot be turned into the equivalent of revelation. Although the Church requires a decision-making process, all the relevant criteria in matters relating to salvation are open to all believers because they are biblical. The biblical portrait of the Church, warts and all, remains foundational in the capacity to inform the minds of those who continue to discern the Church's way in new circumstances.[2]

It is not, however, everything, and the problem with so many appeals to scripture is that they become bogged down in the extremes either of scriptural exegesis and criticism or alternatively of blind fundamentalism. The contention here is that the pattern and example of Jesus are larger than scripture, or creeds, or dogmas, and that it is this pattern and example together with the contemporary presence of the Spirit of Christ in the church, which binds all the other elements (creeds, traditions and so on) together and gives them meaning. It is Jesus Christ (experienced both within these things and within the ongoing life of the church) who 'validates' creeds, Scriptures and traditions, and not vice versa.

To say that the church must base its authority on the pattern of Jesus Christ and on its ability to model its own life on that pattern is merely to make a bald assertion. It remains to establish the precise content of the authority of

Christ and hence of his church, and to see why it is that an appeal to Jesus Christ himself as a source of authority is both a realistic and a coherent one even today.

II

If the church is to locate its own authority in that of Jesus Christ, then clearly we must examine his authority and attempt to establish what was (and is) distinctive about it. That he had authority is not substantially in doubt – the crowds who followed him sensed it and responded to it, and his teaching was even compared favourably with that of the scribes who were the traditional 'authorities' within Judaism: 'When Jesus had finished saying these things, the crowds were amazed at his teaching, because he taught as one who had authority, and not as their teachers of the law' (Matt. 7.28–9). It was, indeed, his authority which contributed in large measure to his death: without authority in his life and teaching he would never have constituted a threat either to Rome or to the leaders of Judaism.

In his arrest, trial and death too, we see the enormous disparity between the concepts of power and authority to which we have paid attention earlier. There is no question of Jesus' powerlessness – events move along with a hideous inexorability towards his gruesome death; but there is equally no question of his authority – before all of his accusers, and in the face of all their power over him, Jesus remains the only figure of complete integrity and therefore of authority, able to show up their duplicity and hatred for what it is.

In his death, then, Jesus displays a radically powerless authority, and it is this same distinctive quality of authority that we may identify throughout the rest of his life and ministry. In her study of authority in the church, Gillian

Evans points to the centrality of this authority without power, and her remarks would apply equally well to the authority of the church:

> The characteristics of Christ's own exercise of authority are the model for the exercise of authority in the Church. He who is Lord of all came as the servant of people's needs. He made no compromise with wrong but he showed infinite compassion for the sinner. He compelled no one to come to him, but he attracted multitudes. On the Cross he exerted no coercive power, but his authority there reached its highest expression. The power which is lodged in the Church must, then, be the paradoxical 'power of the crucified', and that makes it at once fully human and fully divine in its strength in weakness (Ephesians 4), reflecting both the lordship and the service of Christ (Ephesians 4; Philippians 2.11).[3]

The same insistence on the authority of the humility and servanthood of Christ would equally be reflected in the work of other modern thinkers on the nature of Anglicanism.

At the heart of Jesus' authority, then, is this ideal of humility and servanthood, but this is not by itself sufficient fully to explain his distinctive authority. Being humble or being a servant do not themselves constitute a pattern of authority. What does constitute such a pattern are the qualities or values which are expressed by means of this attitude of humility. In other words, given that the humility of Jesus was central to his person and to his task, what were the features of his life and ministry which imparted an authority to that humility?

There are, no doubt, many elements of Jesus' life which might be pointed out, but here I propose to single out just three characteristics which seem to me to be fundamental to any understanding of who Jesus was, and then to suggest that all of these three are dependent upon a fourth – and that these four things taken together constitute, in large measure at least, the grounds for the humble authority of Jesus, and that in so far as the church also conforms to these things they may provide the ground for the humble authority of the church also.

The first of these elements is simply the compassion of Jesus for all those whom he met, regardless of their station in life; regardless of their need; regardless of their religiousness; regardless of their race. All that mattered was that they came to him in their necessity. A number of factors of this all-embracing compassion may be isolated. To begin with it was a compassion which was so integral to Jesus that it simply seemed to flow from him. Jesus never appears to have had to summon up this compassion against his instincts or to dredge it up in spite of a contrary mood. He is approached with some trepidation by a leper: 'Lord, if you are willing, you can make me clean,' and there is no hesitation from Jesus, but the simple reply, 'I am willing; be clean' (Matt. 8.2–3).

Then too, it was a compassion which embraced the needs of both body and soul. Whatever the confusion of memories and successive editings may be which produced the parallel stories of the feeding of the five thousand and the feeding of the four thousand, it is surely significant that in St Mark's Gospel the evangelist relates each incident to a different aspect of Jesus' compassion. In the feeding of the five thousand Mark records his compassion for the need of their souls: 'When Jesus landed and saw a large crowd, he had compassion on them, because they were like sheep without a shepherd. So he began teaching them many things' (Mark 6.34), and in the feeding of the four thousand there is a similar compassion for their physical need: 'During those days another large crowd gathered. Since they had nothing to eat, Jesus called his disciples to him and said, "I have compassion for these people; they have already been with me three days and have nothing to eat. If I send them home hungry, they will collapse on the way, because some of them have come a long distance."' (Mark 8.1–3).

It is also a non-judgmental compassion. Certainly Jesus is harsh about the hypocrisy of certain groups – most especially those who are 'professionally' religious – yet at the same time there is always compassion for the simple needs of those who come to him, regardless of their failings: a compassion most beautifully illustrated in the, admittedly historically uncertain, story of the woman taken in adultery. Whatever the historical status of this story may be, it nonetheless makes plain the Gospel writer's attempt to capture the depth of Jesus' compassion, even for someone whom everyone else was ready to condemn both morally and legally.

Finally, it was a compassion which had the strength to remain undiminished even in the face of suffering and hatred: condemned himself, Jesus yet prays for the forgivenness of his tormentors, and listens to the need for reassurance and hope of one who is similarly condemned. Throughout the life and death of Jesus, then, his every action is underscored by this fundamental attitude of compassion for the needs and the failings of all those whom he came to serve.

The second central element in our understanding of Jesus is his simplicity of life – a simplicity both of style of life and of the direction and orientation of his life. It is exemplified in the stark command, issued by Jesus on so many occasions, of 'Follow me'. For all who heeded this call, it was to be a following which involved going they knew not where, leaving behind all that was familiar and all the security and all the traditions they had known (Luke 9.57–62), and to set out on a journey of wandering and uncertainty, sharing only the simplicity of Jesus' own life and the clear-sighted singleness of purpose which Jesus himself had – a purpose, solely, of doing 'the will of my Father'. In his pursuance of this will, Jesus himself explicitly rejected the possible 'benefits' of his charisma and growing fame, refusing to be acclaimed as a king or a popular leader, and he shows no interest in acquiring anything for himself and teaches his disciples to adopt the same attitude (Matt. 10.8–10).

The third element is closely related to the directional simplicity of Jesus' life, and his sense of being called to do his Father's will, and this is his passionate conviction of the ultimate value of what he did, a sense that the preaching of the kingdom with all that that involved, including the compassion and simplicity referred to here, mattered above all else. Running through the whole of Jesus' ministry there is this certainty – that God, and the relationship of humanity with him, was of supreme importance. This conviction led him to forsake all security and to risk everything, and it led his followers to do likewise. It led him to the utter simplicity of life and purpose to which we have alluded, and it led him constantly to challenge both his disciples and the crowds with the question of where exactly their values and their hearts lay. It is a strand of his ministry which runs right through it from beginning to end: from the story of the child Jesus in the temple, to the cleansing of the temple towards the end of his life. And throughout all of it, his simplicity of life and his passionate singleness of purpose go hand in hand.

There is, though, one further element which fuses all of these together, and which must be seen as the overriding characteristic of Jesus' life and ministry, and hence of his authority. This is, quite simply, that all that Jesus said and did was rooted in a life of prayer and in the depth of his personal relationship with God. From the occasions when the Gospel writers tell us of the prayer of Jesus, it is apparent that this was central to everything else that he did. He sought silence and peace regularly in which to pray, and he draws his disciples aside for the same purpose. At all the major points in his life – whether in his experience of temptation (whatever that was historically) at the start of his ministry, or his forthcoming arrest and trial at the end of it – we see him turning before all else to prayer, and we see him also devoting a substantial amount of his teaching to the subject of prayer and what it means to pray aright. In the course of this teaching, too, he gives his disciples their pattern of prayer with its key-note right at its beginning: 'Our Father...' This relationship with God both inspires and flows from Jesus' life of prayer, and it is in prayer that this relationship reaches its most profound expression. It is in prayer too that Jesus finds the well-springs of his compassion, simplicity of life and conviction. For Jesus, in his life of prayer, God is so present that within a human life the qualities of the divine life are enabled to shine forth, and a human life becomes the channel for the compassion, simplicity and passion of God himself. It is, I believe, within a conformity to this pattern and mind of Christ, and similarly rooted in prayer, that the church may find a new authority – one which will be the humble authority of Christ himself.

III

Having concentrated, in our development of this notion of authority, so much upon the Jesus of the Gospels, it is important to stress, before proceeding further, that a reliance upon Jesus as the locus for authority does not involve any sort of tendency towards a fundamentalist or anti-critical attitude to scripture. That this is so will be outlined more fully in chapter 8, but here it is sufficient to argue that the church's focus on Jesus – a focus primarily on a person not on a dogma – can assimilate (or at least credibly cope with and interpret) all the pluralisms of modern society, precisely because there is a focus on a person and not on any particular attitude to scripture or creeds or dogmas. Our understanding of, and relationship with a person are flexible enough to allow for change and growth in a way that rigid dogmatic formulations are not. Likewise it does not depend on any particular attitude towards scripture, or towards the historical authenticity of any particular passage from the Gospels. It does not matter overmuch whether Jesus did or did not utter this or that saying, or did or did not walk on the water for example. Indeed, very often it would actually make more sense of our understanding of Jesus' human relationship with his heavenly Father if he had not done some of these things as critical biblical scholarship would suggest, for then we see in Jesus a humanity open to the divine, rather than a Greek-style *theios aner* performing clever tricks merely for the sake of astonishing his audience. Finally, in this context, in an authority founded on a turning to the pattern and mind of Christ, there is an appeal not only to the Christ of the Gospels but also to the Christ of Christian experience, and the church's relationship with Christ is therefore once again flexible and open to change and development, and not tied to a rigid once-for-all revelation but rather to the ongoing experience of the church as witnessed to both in scripture itself, in tradition, and in the current life and worship of that church.

Flowing from this, there is also the consequence that a renewed emphasis is placed on the prayer and worship of the church, as being the place where our relationship with God through Christ is mediated and nourished. This is true to the pattern of Christ himself as we have seen, and it also stresses the place of the church's prayer as constituting its

120

characteristic and distinctive mode of life and activity. The importance of this is further enhanced if the Christian life is primarily seen – as we have argued that it should be – as being governed by a relationship and not by a set of dogmatic formulations. Prayer is the life-blood of that relationship: it is the conversation of the human spirit with God. It may be that certain doctrinal ideas are formulated in response to the experience of that relationship, but the relationship itself, and prayer as the place where the Church can both hear and speak of things divine, remain the foundation of all that follows.

With this life of prayer at its heart, and sustained by its living relationship with God through Jesus Christ, the church is then empowered to live after the pattern of Christ, and to reflect in its own life his compassion, simplicity of life and conviction. Indeed in its 'great' figures these are the qualities which the church displays, and which can and do still speak with divine authority even in a sceptical world. From my own province of the Anglican Church, one could point to a figure such as the late Archbishop of Armagh, the Rt Revd George Otto Simms, as exemplifying the truth of this; and were one to risk embarrassing the living, he would be found to be not alone in the contemporary church. The effect of such individuals is incalculable, and the overriding impression which they leave with those whom they meet (and often these are people outside the church) is that they have met with someone immensely special, through whom something beyond the merely human has been mediated. For those who meet them from within a Christian perspective, the impression is even more direct – it is often described as having been an experience of the mediated presence of Christ himself, through whom God is revealed.

Clearly, these figures are the exception rather than the rule, and it would be unrealistic to expect every member of every congregation to exemplify the quite remarkable qualities of these rare individuals. However, I would suggest that the 'authority' which these figures undoubtedly carry does represent a credible model for the church – a model which is available to it on the sole condition that it should learn first to conform to the pattern and mind of Christ as these figures have done in their own individual lives.

The reason, then, that these same figures stand out is that they have done what it is, in theory, the business of the whole church to have done, and the fact that they 'teach with authority and not as the scribes' indicates a major failing on the part of the vast bulk of the church. The reality of this failing is not hard to find. If one looks at the life of almost any church congregation (or of the whole church together) the answer to the question of whether it is a life founded on the pattern and mind of Christ looks, even to fellow believers, and certainly to non-Christians, to be a resounding 'No'. Where are the compassion, simplicity and passion of Christ in most Anglican congregations? It is often hard to see them amidst the passing of resolutions A and B, the condemnation of gays and cohabitees (the publicans and sinners of modern church life), the self-absorbed concern with church finance and personal pensions, and the genteel and refined placing of bottoms on pews which constitutes the heart (or the seat?) of Anglican parochial spirituality. Almost everywhere, admittedly, there are the germs of a life lived according to the pattern of Christ: there are the individual lives in whom the presence of Christ is reflected; and there is the occasional faltering decision of a Parochial Church Council or Vestry in the direction of true and sacrificial compassion or generosity. But so often these individual lives and faltering steps are, in the eyes of the world, eclipsed by the institutionalized and self-preserving attitudes embodied in the majority of the church's life, both individual and corporate.

Similarly, and without wishing at all to denigrate the true holiness which is to be found tucked away in all corners of the Anglican world, where is the passionate life of prayer or vibrancy of worship which so strongly characterized the life of Jesus himself or that of the early church? Our worship is, for the most part, a gentle and dignified discourse with the Almighty in which he is presented with only those things which we believe he would be gratified to have vouchsafed to him. The church does not, in the main, find in its worship and prayer a means of communicating its most heartfelt needs or its deepest passions, nor its sorrows and its furies; and equally it often does not find there the peace and stillness within which the voice of God may be most distinctly heard. God is addressed in the courteous language of genteel piety, and our voices fill the emptiness of that stillness and silence which is the medium of his reply. God himself is silenced by the prayers of his church.

IV

Of all the difficulties, controversies and challenges facing the contemporary church (and certainly the Anglican part of that church), this is, I believe, at once the most formidable and the most vital: the need to find again a whole-hearted relationship with God in worship, in which our human listening may be informed by the silence of divine speech; and from this centre of prayer to live once more the life of Christ incarnate, emulating not in pride his divinity, but in humility his compassion, his simplicity of life, and his passionate conviction of the value of the kingdom of God for the realm of humanity.

The above remarks on the state of the church may appear to be harsh and uncompromising, and the description of the church's call and task may equally appear to be utopian or unrealistic. Such is not, I believe, the case. The essence of the church's call has always been to live a life based upon the pattern of Christ, and to seek to discover within it as its guide and inspiration, the mind of Christ himself. This call has not changed with the passing of the centuries. Instead what has changed is the response of the church: what once looked like a holy calling looks now (in a vision coloured by the sceptical twentieth-century world) like an unrealistic ideal; what was a personal and corporate aim of life looks now like an unattainable dream. The result of this change of perspective is that the church has, I believe, settled for second best. If – as we all acknowledge – it is not possible perfectly to exemplify the mind of Christ, then it is acceptable merely to aim a little higher than my neighbour: he does not attend church and I do; he gives nothing to Oxfam, and I give ten pounds; he does not acknowledge the reality of God, and I at least bow in his direction every Sunday. Sadly, for many Christians, this is the reality of contemporary faith and worship, and I venture to suggest that it is not enough.

If the church (and as a part of it, the Anglican Church) is to recover not only its authority, but also quite simply its credibility, then it has, I believe, to rediscover its devotion to Jesus Christ and its calling to follow in his footsteps. It is from the devotion of this life of Christ-centred prayer, and the following of his call to compassion and servanthood in its own life, that the church can then go forth with authority to the world to proclaim the marvellous truth of the gospel which it is already experiencing and living through the power (*dynamis*) and presence of the risen Christ in its midst. Then, and only then, will the church speak, preach, teach and call men and women to it and to God again with authority – when it lives with humility and in the hand of God, whose *dynamis* (expressed in compassion, simplicity and passion) embraces not only the church itself, but the whole of that world to which the church finds itself called afresh to witness.

8

Further Consequences

I

Any proposal for change in the attitudes or life-style of the church will inevitably produce consequences for the life of that church; and before any change can responsibly be embarked upon it is important at least to attempt to ascertain whether the result of any proposed re-orientation is likely to be for the better or for the worse. Whatever changes may be proposed within the church will always be 'known by their fruits', and these fruits must be shown to be in keeping with the fundamental nature and purpose of the church. If they should ever be shown to be at odds with this nature and purpose, then it may be assumed that the original proposals for change were themselves seriously flawed. Any change of direction or orientation must represent an addition to, and not a detraction from the church's traditional understanding of its calling and work.

The proposed re-orientation in the present work is no exception. Thus the question must be asked: are the present proposals for identifying a new locus of authority and identity for the church in the person and work of Jesus Christ such as to enhance rather than to diminish the church's perception of its holy calling? And similarly, are the emphases on the fundamental calling to prayer, and to a participation in the ongoing qualities of the life and ministry of Christ such as to be faithful to the nature of, and to build up the distinctive identity and authority of the church's life?

In answer to this question I would simply suggest three things: one of which concerns the dynamic of faith – its vibrancy and life; one of which concerns the consequences for the role and status of doctrine within the life of the church; and the final one of which concerns the church's life of prayer and worship. If the re-orientation of the church's attitude proposed here can satisfy the various different criteria demanded by these areas of the church's life, then it is a re-orientation which is worthy of serious consideration by the church.

II

First, then, there is the consequence for the life and dynamism of the church and of the Christian faith. We have argued for a more person-based faith which is rooted in the Jesus of the Gospels and in the Jesus of ongoing Christian experience in the church. This has, I believe, the consequence that faith becomes more immediate and more alive. People are capable of being inspired by a wide variety of things, and it must be acknowledged that among them are creeds and dogmas and ideologies. At the same time, however, it is also true that none of these has ever acted as an inspiration and a source of life and value in the same way that a personal relationship or a personal loyalty have done. Jesus, even as imprisoned in creeds and dogmas, is still capable of inspiring the church; but that same Jesus once set free to be loved and followed in himself is incomparably a greater source of life and devotion for the church and for the individuals who comprise it. I can say, 'I believe in Jesus Christ our Lord', and mean it, but the effect of that is as nothing compared with the experience of that same Jesus Christ as risen and present in my private prayer and in the corporate worship of the church. There, and there alone, is the love which raises my human love to something which I can believe may overcome my human irritations and dislikes; there, and there alone, is a compassion which can rise above my human frustration with my fellow creatures and tinge our lives with the hues of divinity.

The centrality of the person of Jesus, rather than of any particular dogmatic formulation about him, is thus an emphasis which is at least likely to revitalize the faith of the church and impart a new impetus to it. It is also an emphasis which is, importantly, in keeping with much that Anglicanism holds dear. It is consonant with the understanding of the early church, for whom specific dogmas were only gradually extrapolated out of their experience of the Jesus whom the apostles had known and whom they experienced as living in their midst. Similarly, too, it is fully in keeping with the traditional Anglican attitude towards scripture – that is, not a slavish or exclusive one, but one which is reinforced both by tradition and by reason: that is, both by the traditions and present experience of Christ in the church, and by the church's mature reflection both on scripture itself and on that ongoing experience. A new emphasis on the place of Jesus at the heart of faith is therefore at once in keeping with the past, and a sign of new life for the present.

Secondly, there is a consequence for the position of doctrine within the church, and this is a particularly sensitive area within Anglicanism. The Anglican Church may have prided itself (misguidedly, some would suggest) on supposedly having no specific doctrines of its own, but it has equally prided itself on having a more than usually thoughtful approach to faith, and a great understanding of, and respect for the doctrines of the first five centuries of the Christian church. Anything, therefore, which even remotely threatens to re-evaluate any of this heritage must be assessed and evaluated very carefully indeed. It is true, then, that in the move from dogma to personality there is an implied consequence for the status of dogma and doctrine: it becomes something of the second order rather than the first order, but this does not, as we shall see, necessarily devalue it or make it irrelevant.

First, however, it is important to identify the more obviously positive gains of this move. We have already argued that one consequence is a revitalized faith, and flowing from this is the fact that doctrine can now be read back into experience. It is not necessary to 'pump up' the present experience of the church by appealing to doctrine to discover what that experience should mean: but rather, if the church is aware of a living experience of Christ and of the presence of God, then doctrine becomes a framework to help us to interpret that experience. This is by no means a new concept. There is a perfect example, often overlooked, in Romans 1, in which St Paul introduces his letter by referring to his understanding of Jesus Christ:

> Paul, a servant of Christ Jesus, called to be an apostle and set apart for the gospel of God – the gospel he promised beforehand through his prophets in the Holy Scriptures regarding his Son, who as to his human nature was a descendant of David, and who through the Spirit of holiness was declared with power to be the Son of God, by his resurrection from the dead: Jesus Christ our Lord.

Here, St Paul confers on Jesus what might be called a 'retrospective divinity'. St Paul does not enter into the niceties of Greek metaphysics, or try to work out how Jesus' divine and human natures can philosophically coinhere. Instead he looks to the events of Jesus' life and reads them in the light of his death and resurrection – a light which casts the shadow of divinity back over all that went before, without losing itself in ineffable speculation.

Such a doctrinal method, if followed, allows Christianity (as we argued briefly in the previous chapter) to become infinitely flexible in its response to the world without ever abandoning its basic conviction as to the centrality of Jesus Christ and his place as the locus of God's self-revelation to humankind. We are set free from the shackles of rigid doctrinal formulations (which as relativism rightly acknowledges are always cast in the mould and language of a particular age and culture) and allowed to formulate our own more provisional (and therefore more meaningful) estimates of how and what we can rightly be said to believe.

As we noted previously, however, this does not detract from the significance of Christian doctrine. It may be logically secondary to experience, and it may be more provisional, but our understanding of doctrine still represents the fruit of Christian reflection on the church's experience, and as such, whatever conclusions may be reached will still help to inform – although they will not, of course, entirely govern – that experience in the future. Doctrine remains a valuable check on the excesses which are otherwise liable to creep into Christian faith and practice, and offers a framework of meaning within which any claimed experience may be tested and evaluated. Doctrine thus retains a significant place within the Christian faith, but finds itself at once challenged and re-invigorated by being drawn into a new and creative relationship with the riches of Christian experience past and present, and made flexible enough to respond to the questions presented to it by other disciplines in a philosophically and epistemologically rapidly changing world.

Thirdly, there is a major consequence (as was touched upon in the previous chapter) for the church's life of prayer and worship: that it is enhanced and invested with an even greater value than previously. We have already seen the reasons for this in terms of the primacy of prayer in maintaining and nourishing our relationship with God through Jesus Christ, and here the purpose is merely to indicate that this renewed attention to prayer and worship is fully in keeping with some of the deepest convictions of Anglicanism, as also is a renewed intimation of the awesomeness of what it is that we do in prayer and in the celebration of the sacraments.

My own first reminder of this awesome quality which surrounds, or should surround, our worship was given to me by a retired priest in the days following my ordination to the priesthood. Canon George Lamb, seeing the enthusiasm and almost over-careful preparation by the young priest for worship, said to me some words which I have carried with me ever since: 'Never grow so familiar with it all that you start to handle holy things lightly,' and he explained that one of the greatest sorrows of his life was to see either priests or congregations who had lost their sense of reverence and just 'did' worship in the same way as one does the shopping.

A similar warning from a more well-known voice would be that issued by Stephen Sykes:

It would be spectacularly inappropriate to our age to become casual in our preparation to receive the Holy Communion. At the heart of the modern refusal to recognize the point of emphasizing the fact of unworthiness and the real ground of worthiness lies a disinclination to consider the holiness of God. We misunderstand the nature of God's love if we view it as no more than avuncular tolerance, in the presence of which we can be presumptuously casual. Such an attitude mirrors all too well a contemporary cultural style. Herbert, on the other hand, shows us a priest 'in great confusion' especially at Communion times, 'as being not only to receive God, but to break and administer him'.

That such breath-taking language might co-exist with intimacy and a sense of one's own comic absurdity has everything to do with our understanding of grace. 'Cheap grace' remains, as Bonhoeffer maintained, an abiding temptation to the professionally religious.[1]

If, then, a renewed emphasis on the primacy of our relationship with God through Jesus Christ leads us also – as it should – to an enrichment of our life of prayer and recalls us to the magnitude and majesty of our task of worship, then this is a development to be welcomed by Anglicanism as belonging to its own very heart and soul.

As with many large and historical organizations, the church is intrinsically conservative and has an inbuilt resistance to change, and it may be that any proposal which involves change will find it difficult to receive a hearing from the church. However, in each of the three potential consequences which we have outlined there is, as well as an acknowledged need for certain changes of expectation and attitude, also a real possibility of gain for the church if these changes can be made and assimilated within the life of the church. It appears that perhaps the time has come when a re-appraisal of the church's orientation such as we have advocated, may be in the first instance life-saving and thereafter life-enhancing.

Conclusion

This study has concerned itself principally with some of the problems confronting Anglicanism, and in particular with the issue of precisely what kind of authority the Anglican Church can credibly claim for its life and its witness. The discussion has been conducted from within a specifically Anglican context, but many of the reflections on what it means to be the church, and on the nature of the church's life based on that of its Lord and Master Jesus Christ, would be equally in place in a discussion of any other part of the church catholic.

In our present divided state of Christendom it seems unlikely that the whole church will come jointly to a common mind on any of the issues which confront it, and we can only hope that each Communion will learn from the others as each of us takes one or another step, whether confident or faltering, towards fulfilling our mutual calling to be God's holy people offering themselves in love for the service of the world.

The pattern of life outlined here is one that is offered for Anglicans, and there is no reason why our Anglican response to the issues raised here should not be a part of our witness to the whole church, from which other Communions may draw inspiration for their own journey with God. As Stephen Sykes comments:

Conclusion

The problems for the Church of England are mostly those common to the whole Church, and we must learn to look not sideways to left and right, but forwards to the future, confident that God can call even English Anglicans to set an example of what it means to be faithful and obedient to the vision of his kingdom.[1]

It is my own firm belief that it is within the pattern of the life of Christ, and by seeking his mind through a renewed commitment to prayer and worship, that Anglicanism may find both this vision of the kingdom and the *dynamis* of God himself, whence will flow within the life of the church and through it to the world, the humble authority of the Christ who was, and is, at once both king of all and servant of all. That, at least, remains my hope and my prayer.

Notes

Introduction

1. Stephen Sykes, *Unashamed Anglicanism*, Darton Longman & Todd 1995, p.xvi.

2. See, for example, Stephen Sykes (ed), *Authority in the Anglican Communion*, Toronto 1987.

3. G. R. Evans, *Authority in the Church: a Challenge for Anglicans,* The Canterbury Press 1990, p.19.

4. John Hick, *An Interpretation of Religion*, Macmillan 1989, pp.207–8.

5. Stephen Sykes, *Unashamed Anglicanism*, pp.119–20.

6. *For the Sake of the Kingdom*, Anglican Consultative Council 1986. Quoted in Sykes, *Unashamed Anglicanism*, p.120.

7. A prime example might be the Donatists, who kept themselves as a pure unspotted church.

8. Luke 4. 17–19 (NIV).

1 Historical Authority

1. Alexander Pope, *An Essay on Man*, Epistle i, l.289.

2. Sydney Smith, *Memoirs and Letters of the Revd Sydney Smith*, Vol.I (1855), p.204.

Notes

2 Structural Authority

1. G. R. Evans, *Authority in the Church*, p.xi.

2. Ignatius, *The Epistle to the Ephesians* in *The Ante-Nicene Fathers*, Alexander Roberts & James Donaldson (eds), Wm. B. Eerdmans, Grand Rapids 1981, p.50.

3. Ibid., p.51.

4. Eusebius, Letter to his Church, quoted in J. Stevenson (ed), *A New Eusebius*, SPCK 1957, pp.364–8.

5. The Irish *Book of Common Prayer*, p.297.

6. *Alternative Occasional Offices*, General Synod of the Church of Ireland 1993, p.114.

7. Ibid., p.145.

8. James Woodforde, *The Diary of a Country Parson, 1758–1802*, John Beresford (ed), OUP 1978, p.61.

9. Ibid., p.231.

10. Ian R. Boyd, 'What are the Clergy For? Clerical Role Uncertainty and the State of Theology' in *Theology*, May/June 1995, pp.187–96.

11. SCM Press 1994.

3 Biblical and Doctrinal Authority

1. Don Cupitt, *Taking Leave of God*, SCM Press 1980; David A. Hart, *Faith in Doubt*, Mowbrays 1994.

2. Tim Peacock, 'Faith and Reason – A Casualty?' in *The Church of Ireland Gazette*, 26 August 1994, p.13.

3. The Irish *Book of Common Prayer*, p.57.

4. *Alternative Occasional Offices*, The General Synod of the Church of Ireland 1993, p.114.

5. Ibid., p.145.

6. Charles Darwin, *Autobiography*. Quoted in Christopher Ralling (ed), *The Voyage of Charles Darwin*, BBC 1978, p.162.

7. Don Cupitt, *The Worlds of Science and Religion*, Sheldon Press 1976, pp.102–3.

8. For a fuller treatment of Cupitt's development see Stephen Ross White, *Don Cupitt and the Future of Christian Doctrine*, SCM Press 1993, Part I.

9. Stephen Sykes, *Unashamed Anglicanism*, pp.xv–xvi.

4 Moral Authority

1. 'The Order for the Visitation of the Sick' from *The Book of Common Prayer*, 1662.

2. Ibid.

3. Dorothee Soelle, *Theory for Sceptics*, Mowbray 1995, p.85.

4. Ibid., p.86.

5. Ibid.

6. Ibid.

7. Ibid., pp.86–7.

8. *Something to Celebrate*, published for the Church of England Board of Social Responsibility by Church House Publishing 1995.

5 Anglicanism in Crisis

1. Stephen Sykes, *Unashamed Anglicanism*, pp.214–15.

2. Ibid., p.213.

Notes

6 Authority or Power?

1. *The Lambeth Conference 1948* (London 1948), Report No. IV, 'The Anglican Communion', pp.84–5. Quoted in Stephen Sykes, *Unashamed Anglicanism*, pp.168–9.

2. Stephen Sykes, *Unashamed Anglicanism*, p.169.

3. Ibid., pp.174–5.

4. Ibid., p.159.

7 A New Authority

1. *The Lambeth Conference 1948*, Report No. IV, op cit.

2. Stephen Sykes, *Unashamed Anglicanism*, p.131.

3. G. R. Evans, *Authority in the Church*, p.18.

8 Further Consequences

1. Stephen Sykes, *Unashamed Anglicanism*, pp.61–2.

Conclusion

1. Stephen Sykes, *Unashamed Anglicanism*, pp.176–7.

Index of Names